Helping Your Chemically Dependent Teenager Recover

A Guide for Parents and Other Concerned Adults

Peter R. Cohen, M.D.

JOHNSON INSTITUTE®
Minneapolis

Library of Congress Cataloging-in-Publishing Data
Cohen, Peter R.
Helping your chemically dependent teenager recover: A guide for parents and other concerned adults / Peter R. Cohen.
    p. cm.
Includes bibliographical references and index.
    ISBN 1-56246-015-3
    1. Teenagers—Drug use. 2. Teenagers—Alcohol use. 3. Narcotic addicts—Rehabilitation. 4. Alcoholic—Rehabilitation. 5. Drug abuse—Relapse—Prevention. 6. Alcoholism—Relapse—Prevention. 7. Parents and teenager.
I. Title.
HV5824. Y68C62 1911
649'.4 - dc20

                        91-16558
                        CIP

Printed in the United States of America

91 92 93 94 95 96 / 6 5 4 3 2 1

Acknowledgments

Many people deserve thanks for their help in creating this book:

My wife Susan, who gets the gold medal for her love, intelligence, humor, patience, and honesty.

My children Shari, Debby, and Danny for their love, intelligence, respect, as well as the ability to keep their father humble.

My mother and father, who taught me about the joy of living and learning, about courage and commitment, and about believing that you can survive anything.

John Meeks, M.D., for being a selfless and giving teacher and mentor and for providing helpful comments about this book.

Richard Schwartz, M.D., for his commitment to research, inspiration, energy and persistence.

The Psychiatric Institute of Montgomery County, Straight Incorporated, Whale's Tales and Karma House in Pittsburgh, Pennsylvania, Karma Academy for Boys and Girls, and the Fairbridge Residential Program, for the spirit and support they give to troubled teenagers and their families. These excellent programs are "co-authors" of this book.

Thomas Poon, C.A.C., and Debby Riley, M.A., who by force of their personalities, professional efforts, and friendship are great healers and teachers.

Miriam Polster, Ph.D., Joseph Zinker, Ph.D., Sonia Nevis, Ph.D., and Maxwell Boverman, M.D., who teach that earning the qualities of honesty and courage takes hard work, creativity, and playfulness.

The late Ken Williams, M.D., who was a pioneer in teaching psychiatric trainees to appreciate the illness of chemical dependence.

Lenore Franzen, Cynthia Peterson, and James Bitney of the Johnson Institute for their editorship, their creativity, and their infinite patience.

Carole Remboldt of the Johnson Institute, Susan Barnhill, C.A.C., and Paul Henry, M.Div., who were responsible for the genesis of this book.

Peter Luongo, Ph.D., who, while creating this country's most dynamic public mental health program for children and adolescents, took the time to comment on the shaping of this book.

Todd Estroff, Ph.D., for his ideas and teachings about adolescent chemical dependence and dual diagnosis.

Vernon Johnson, Terence Gorski, Stephanie Brown, Gordon Marlatt, Sharon Wegscheider-Cruse, and Claudia Black for their pioneering ideas in the field of recovery.

The families who volunteered their time to share with me their stories of recovery. Their sharing has influenced this book.

Finally, thanks to the many teens and families who have the courage to seek help. Their patience and willingness to be vulnerable are more than admirable. I thank them for teaching me how to help them find contentment and integrity.

Contents

INTRODUCTION

Ten years ago parents with chemically dependent children were lucky if they could find a program that understood adolescent chemical dependence and knew how to evaluate and treat these teenagers. Typically, adolescents would be put into a program designed for adults. Even after months of treatment, many teenagers failed to stay sober. This concerned a few pioneering professionals and parents. They rethought how teenage chemical dependence should be treated, and they developed new programs that offered help for dependent teens and their families, whose health and well-being had been seriously threatened by alcohol and other drug use.[1]

---

[1] Note that the term "alcohol or other drugs" is used throughout this book to emphasize that alcohol is a drug—just like tranquilizers, cocaine, marijuana, heroin, or any other mind-altering substance. The book also uses the term "chemical dependence" because it covers dependence on all these mind-altering drugs and because it's inclusive, short, and simple. Too often people talk about "alcohol or drugs" or "alcohol and drugs" as if alcohol were somehow different from drugs and in a category by itself. True, our culture, our government, even our laws, treat alcohol differently from the way they treat other drugs such as pot, crack, or smack. But the symptoms of dependence are essentially the same for all these mind-altering drugs, and there is an urgent need to find ways to prevent or intervene with their use.

By the mid-1980s, public education had led to an increase in the number of treatment programs, allowing more adolescents to get help. But a new problem arose. These teenagers seemed more disturbed than those of the past. The term "dual diagnosis" was coined to describe the problem. In addition to their dependence on chemicals, these teens also often suffered from depression, emotional, physical, or sexual abuse, learning problems, attention deficits, and other disorders. Clinicians also discovered that some families had similar problems going back over many generations. Again, the professionals were faced with the challenge of finding appropriate care and treatment for these teens and their families.

Helping Your Chemically Dependent Teenager Recover is written for the parent whose child has serious problems with alcohol or other drugs. It recognizes the need for both teenager and parent to recover from the disease of chemical dependence. Understand that with chemical dependence there are no guarantees that your teen will never use again. But also understand that recovery is a process that offers you and your teenager a better life and much hope for the future.

ADOLESCENCE AND DEVELOPMENT

We tend to fool ourselves into thinking that adolescents are young adults because of the ways they look and behave. But teenagers aren't adults; they have a unique path of development. You're raising someone whose body and brain are rapidly changing. Your adolescent is still trying to make sense out of his or her values, emotions, behaviors, and friendships. This is a time for developing a healthy identity. Having an identity means that a person becomes more secure and certain about long-term goals, career, healthy friendships, sexuality, religious and moral values, and group loyalties.

A chemically dependent teenager is a child trapped in an adult body, trying unsuccessfully to grow into an adult. Such a child has a poorly formed or empty identity that is based on his or her ability to find and use alcohol or other drugs. Every day of using postpones the child's growth toward a mature identity. This is why it takes chemically dependent teenagers so long to "get their act together."

During your child's recovery you may have a hard time knowing what's normal for teenagers, let alone what to expect. Teens can show the strangest, funniest, goofiest, most frightening, endearing, and loving behaviors, all in a single day. An adolescent needs to try on new behaviors to find out what fits his or her personality. This is part of the natural process of growing up. Until you can figure out the meaning of your child's behavior, be patient during his or her recovery, and expect to see a variety of behaviors.

For some young people, the prospect of growing up in addition to recovering is too much. They would rather go back to the days of innocence before they had a problem with alcohol or other drugs. They think they can simply start over. Unfortunately, they can never return to what was; but they can create a life that is fulfilling and meaningful, a life that allows them full independence.

For recovering teens, growing up is a particular challenge. They must move from depending on chemicals, to depending on others for staying sober, to finding a balance between depending on oneself and depending on others. A teenager needs to move gradually toward independence from you, at a pace he or she can handle, given the stage of his or her recovery. You and your teen will most likely have many battles over the problem of dependence versus independence. Remember to listen openly and be sensitive to your teenager's fears that he or she may never experience the independence that we, as adults, enjoy and value so much.

Another challenge may confront your child. He or she may not be emotionally or intellectually ready to come to grips with trying to regain control of a life that is very much out of control. But it is only when a chemically dependent person admits that he or she is absolutely powerless and out of control that recovery begins. Only then can that person move from an unhealthy dependence on chemicals to a healthy dependence on self and others.

STAGES OF RECOVERY

I have identified four stages of recovery for chemically dependent adolescents, which are discussed in detail in Chapters 1-4: (1) crisis control, (2) stability and structure, (3) consistency and balance, and (4) attachment. As you read this book, identify what stage of recovery your son or daughter is in. For some of you, your teenager might be showing early signs of having a problem with alcohol or other drugs. For others, your child may have already begun treatment but is struggling to stay sober.

Why does it take so long to recover? First, alcohol and other drugs directly harm the way the brain handles thinking, feeling, behaving, and relating. Once a person becomes sober, it may take months for the brain to recover. Some functions don't return easily because of the type of drug and the length of time the person has used it. Marijuana, for example, can impair problem-solving skills for years after a person stops using it. Another reason why recovery is a long process is that it normally takes time for a person to make changes in his or her personality and behavior. People prefer to keep their lives stable and without change, even if change promises a better life. New behavior is risky and might lead to worse circumstances.

When you understand that your child's recovery will be slow but steady, you can feel more at peace and more secure with the job awaiting you. Then you won't expect more rapid growing from your teen than is possible. With each stage of recovery you'll learn what to expect and what specific tasks you must set for yourself in order to ensure a long-lasting recovery.

WHY IT'S WORTH THE EFFORT

You may already have asked yourself, "Will anything really make a difference? How can our lives get better after all that has happened to us?" I want to assure you that your hard work *will* make a difference, both for your teenager and for yourself. You will discover that your pain will gradually subside, family relationships will grow stronger, and your role as a parent will be recognized by your teenager, perhaps for the first time.

This book will help you in the healing process that lies ahead by encouraging you to educate yourself about recovery, to work hard and take new risks, to experience being successful as a parent, and to keep up your spirits. Helping your teenager recover from chemical dependence is the most loving thing you, as a parent, can do. In the following seven chapters, you'll find a step-by-step guide on how to do this most important of jobs.

CHAPTER 1

STAGE ONE: CRISIS CONTROL

Something is wrong in your family. Daily problems explode into catastrophes. Simple disagreements rapidly deteriorate into shouting matches and near brawls. The normal generation gap between you and your teen has widened to a chasm. You suspect that these problems might stem from your teen's use of alcohol or other drugs, but he or she denies it. You want to help but don't know how. Or you offer your help, but your teen denies he or she needs it. You, your teenager, and, indeed, your whole family are living in a state of crisis, and it's mighty scary! Everything seems out of control. You feel powerless. This means that you're feeling the way people *should* feel when they recognize and admit that there's a problem.

Remember, recovery from chemical dependence can begin only when you realize and admit that you're powerless, and in a crisis situation that seems beyond your control. You can't restore order to your family life if you can't recognize that your family is living in chaos. You won't become a healthy family until you recognize that chemical dependence is a disease that's hurting all of you.[2] That's why the first stage of genuine recovery is called Crisis Control. It's the stage in which you and your teenager begin to realize that you need help that's beyond your resources as a family, the help that chemical dependence treatment can provide.

As mentioned above, no one likes living in the state of crisis. As parents, you will want to move yourselves, your teen, and your family *out* of the Crisis Control Stage and into getting some help as quickly as possible. Moving effectively through the Crisis Control Stage, however, means becoming willing to grapple with what is happening to your family and accepting that your love for a troubled child who seems distant and uninterested in your help will be sorely tested.

In this chapter, we'll look at the problems your teenager faces in this stage and the behaviors your child will likely exhibit as he or she tries to cope with these problems. Then we'll discuss the consequent problems you, as parents, face. Finally, we'll outline four specific tasks that will help you and your family get out of Crisis Control and into getting professional help.

---

[2] It was once believed that chemical dependence was a sign of low self-control, lax morals, irresponsibility, or some other character flaw. Chemically dependent people were told to "shape up" and "get it together," or they were dismissed as "sinners," "weak-willed," or "just that way."

Today we know better: *Chemical dependence is a disease.* In fact, The American Medical Association, American Psychiatric Association, American Public Health Association, American Hospital Association, American Psychological Association, National Association of Social Workers, World Health Organization, and the American College of Physicians have all officially pronounced alcoholism as a disease. In April of 1987, the American Society of Addiction Medicine—whose membership includes over 3,500 doctors certified as specialists in chemical dependence—declared that *what is true for alcoholism is also true for addiction to other drugs.*

It's important to understand and accept that chemical dependence is indeed a disease. Doing so will help relieve your guilt and fear. No one is to blame for another person's chemical dependence. If someone close to you is chemically dependent, you didn't cause it. Furthermore, you can't control it, and you can't cure it.

THE PROBLEMS YOUR TEENAGER FACES

Usually, in the Crisis Control Stage everyone but the teenager will be asking for help. Why is this? First of all, alcohol and other drugs disable the brain and impair a person's ability to control his or her thinking, feeling, or behavior. A chemically dependent adolescent can't experience *deep* feelings of anger, sadness, fear, or shame. He or she wants only to avoid feeling "bad." So, this teen can't sit still in school, think clearly, or study well. Likewise, the dependent teen doesn't care much about anything, because the high from chemicals makes the pressures of life unimportant.

Your teen's friends also can be a problem during the Crisis Control Stage, because friends—even friends who don't use chemicals—support this chaotic way of living. They help the teen fight against or avoid the moral authority of family, school, and society. Young people involved in this kind of fighting or avoidance never criticize their own behavior. Thus, they never have to feel "bad." Unfortunately, they also never develop any real moral sense.

If your teen has a job, that, too, can be a problem. Being employed makes it easier for your teen to buy alcohol and other drugs. But employment soon suffers. Many times your teen is too disorganized to show up regularly or on time for work, so he or she gets fired. Still, your teenager needs and wants the chemicals, so he or she turns to stealing or to "bumming" money from others to get what he or she needs.

Finally, your teen will, in all likelihood, have problems dealing with the real world. Alcohol and other drugs make the user so dysfunctional that he or she isn't in touch with the real world. Living in an *unreal* world makes your teen believe that he or she is in control, *is* powerful. Put simply, chemical use has disabled your child from facing the tasks and challenges of real life. Your teen can't truly care about what's going on around him or her. Alcohol or other drugs have numbed any true emotional pain, and your teen feels fine, even though his or her life is in shambles.

Behaviors to Expect from Your Teenager

Given those problems of a chemically dependent teen, it's hard for parents to understand how such a teenager could still view his or her world as an exciting one. Life is filled with questions and discoveries, accomplishments and challenges. At the same time, the adolescent's world is fraught with confusion and unsettledness. Physiological changes take place rapidly. Emotional changes, or mood swings (from surges of emotion to periods of fatigue), also abound. Parents lose their influence, while the sway of peer groups escalates. Social interests—fun and games—prevail. Conformity seems much safer than individuality. Adolescents pay close attention to matters of dress, make-up, music, hair style, "in" slang—all those things that leave parents scratching their heads.

When teens are at the mercy of erratic and sometimes uncontrollable feelings, when peer pressure is overwhelming, when bodies change, voices crack, and faces break out, teens need help accepting that they're cared for and deserving of care. And they need to know that they're capable of caring for others. They need to experience self-worth and acceptance. And they need all this in order to develop individually as well as socially, to find their own identity and become "who they are," rather than just "one of them."

Oddly enough, help for teens can come only from those people they seem most at odds with—adults. Teens need adults who listen and care about their ideas and feelings, disappointments and dreams. To balance the unsettledness of adolescence, teens look to "settled" adults—and especially to parents—to provide limits, consistency, and understanding. Their self-doubts need to be met with assurance and affirmation. Even when they rebel, teens trust adults to give them guidelines to follow, to make them accountable, and to have confidence in them.

Tragically, when alcohol and other drugs become part of the adolescent development equation, the whole process is affected. When teens turn from caring adults to chemicals to help them deal with their problems, often troublesome but normal types of adolescent behavior worsen.

As you and your teen enter into the Crisis Control Stage of recovery, it's crucial that you understand this. What are these behaviors? Parents of chemically dependent adolescents who have been through the Crisis Control Stage have generally identified the following seven behaviors:

- Depression
- Self-centeredness
- Emotional turbulence
- Disorganization
- Antisocial behavior
- Losing touch
- Frightening behavior

The teenager who is dependent on chemicals very often exhibits one or more of these behaviors to a greater degree than a normal, healthy teen would.

Depression. All teens have periods of moodiness or depression. The chemically dependent teenager usually withdraws from family and friends, actively consider suicide, and sleeps and eats too little or too much. Poor concentration can lead to failing grades in school. This youngster usually looks sad and is able to perk up only for a few hours when with friends. He or she may play music that sounds somber or is overly loud. Unable to deal with anxiety, the young person tries to avoid it by simply clamming up, by keeping secret her or his thoughts and feelings. Know, however, that depression in a chemically dependent teen may not show up until after detoxification (while alcohol and other drugs are being removed from the body), when his or her body is free of drugs.

Self-centeredness. Adolescents act selfishly now and then. But chemically dependent teens can become very self-centered. Involvement with chemicals often drives teenagers to view themselves as more clever and creative than others, to believe that their values alone are noble, and to regard adults and their peers as phonies and hypocrites (except, perhaps, for a small group of like-minded and like-using friends). Usually, these young people don't realize how their behavior affects others, and they can't admit their own mistakes.

Emotional Turbulence. As was mentioned above, the world of the teenager is filled with unsettledness. Life often seems an emotional roller coaster ride. For the chemically dependent adolescent, the roller coaster never stops. High drama is the rule. Because of bickering, the chemically dependent teen has a difficult time sustaining friendships, experiences radical mood swings, and jumps from one intense romance to another. This teen may overdose on pills, slit his wrists, or injure herself in another way, all the while denying attempted suicide.

Disorganization. It's not uncommon for teens to feel and act disorganized now and again. Parents and teachers expect more of them and require them to be more responsible than when they were children. It's also true that a teen's problem with hyperactivity, distractions, a poor attention span, or a learning disability may have its roots in childhood, prior to any chemical use. Clearly, however, chemical dependence can both cause disorganization and worsen a preexisting childhood problem.

Antisocial Behavior. Does your teen try to communicate by arguing and throwing insults? Is your young person's room a mess, clothes inappropriate or in disarray, and music too loud? Does your teen routinely violate rules at home, in school, and in the community? Do you find yourself being inconsistent about rules or giving up on rules altogether because your teen refuses to obey them? In other words, has your teen "crossed over the line" into unacceptable behavior like Josh in the example below?

> *Josh comes home two hours past his curfew, sneaks upstairs, and throws up in the bathroom. Mom says, "Josh, we love you very much, but you're on restriction for the rest of the school year." The very next night Josh deals with this attempt at limit-setting by getting into an argument with Dad, then retreats to his room. When his parents are asleep, he sneaks out of the house to see his friends. In the middle of the night,*

the police call Josh's parents. Josh has been charged with breaking and entering a car, possession of marijuana, and resisting arrest.

A healthy teen may push or bend—but will rarely or consistently break—family, school, or community rules. But if your teen refuses to accept and consistently ignores reasonable social rules (like curfews, school attendance, or safe driving habits), his or her behavior has become very antisocial.

You should know that an adolescent's chronic antisocial behavior may stem not only from chemical use, but from any number of psychiatric problems: for instance, clinical depression, psychosis, physical or sexual abuse, learning disabilities. Likewise, some antisocial teens may have abnormal brain functioning due to head injuries or childbirth injuries.

All this is *not* to say that chemically dependent teens need a psychiatric problem as an excuse to use alcohol or other drugs. Rather, it's simply to point out that about 20 percent of chemically dependent teens are what are called "dual diagnoses." In other words, in addition to chemical dependence, they have some kind of psychiatric disorder that must be dealt with while the teen is in treatment in order to help prevent relapse.

In conclusion, know that not every chemically dependent teenager acts as an antisocial troublemaker like Josh. However, with a little help from their friends, many chemically dependent teens do manage to get themselves into trouble at school, work, or with the law. If your teen exhibits antisocial behavior, it may stem from chemical dependence. And if your teen is chemically dependent, the disease will heighten antisocial behavior.

Losing Touch. Have you heard yourself make any of the following remarks about your teen?

- "He seems to be living in another world."
- "She used to be such a good student, but now she does nothing."

- "He talks about really strange things: blood, death, the emptiness of the universe."
- "She told her friends she's having hallucinations."

Comments like these may indicate that your child is losing touch with reality.

When a teen acts as if he or she is out of touch with reality, the youngster may be suffering from a psychotic condition. At the same time, however, know that excessive use of synthetic hallucinogens such as LSD or PCP can also cause such behavior.

Frightening Behavior. Have you ever been genuinely frightened by your teen's behavior? Chemically dependent teenagers are often openly hostile or cruel. They seem to derive pleasure from the suffering of others or from frightening others with bizarre clothing, destructive behavior, and crude language. A teen who exhibits such behavior may have longstanding but hidden feelings of powerlessness and rage. He or she may also be involved in satanic cults. However, be aware that a teen's involvement with PCP, cocaine, or alcohol can also cause such behavior.

As you try to move yourselves, your teen, and your family out of the Crisis Control Stage and into getting professional help, your child may display any or all of these seven behaviors. Don't panic. Remember, when your child is dependent on chemicals, he or she is out of control. Your teen finds it easier to act out of control than to strive for the strength necessary to communicate better with you. In fact, your child may look at acting out of control as a matter of survival. Such behaviors keep your teen from feeling put down, laughed at, despondent, guilty, or ashamed. Your teen fears that your desire to help—to move him or her into treatment—is but another way of being humiliated and shamed. So your teen resists.

As a matter of fact, you should probably be skeptical of a teen in the Crisis Control Stage who never acts out or who readily agrees without resistance to treatment for chemical abuse. To consider their going along with the treatment idea as mature behavior is a mistake. Experience has taught us that adolescents who promptly ask for treatment at this earliest stage of recovery aren't really admitting their personal powerlessness or lack of control. Rather, they're claiming false control and power by telling themselves, "If I give in and admit to a problem now, I can sit back and not have to work to solve it."

THE PROBLEMS PARENTS FACE

If your teen has problems during this first stage of recovery, you will, too. When your child resists help, yet continues to use alcohol or other drugs, you'll feel desperate and worried. Initially, then, the Crisis Control Stage makes you, as parents, feel helpless. You may even find yourselves denying that your child has a chemical problem or hoping that it's merely a passing adolescent phase. Family members may argue bitterly about how best to deal with that naughty child in their midst. Sometimes intense disagreements, fatigue, and lack of private time may combine to lead some couples to fight often or to even consider divorcing.

Second, parents also experience problems with lack of "staying power." After trying to deal with their "problem child," parents have little energy left to deal with other family members and friends. Not being able to distance themselves from the problem, parents complain to each other instead of reaching out to each other for help and support. Soon, they begin to feel disconnected from each other.

Third, parents may also experience money problems. Less money goes to family necessities and more goes to pay bills stemming from your teen's disease: for example, bills to repair the car he or she wrecked while driving under the influence; bills for the attorney who defended your child against the charge of cocaine possession; bills for counseling or treatment.

Fourth, parents can't deal with the problem of recovery alone. To help their chemically dependent youngster, some families become involved in all kinds of counseling or therapy. Parents and other family members often want fast answers and instant solutions to the problems of their troubled and trouble-making child. When answers or solutions don't come fast enough, or when recovery isn't instantaneous, parents complain, "We've tried everything, and nothing works," and they want to give up.

Don't allow the possibility or the presence of these problems to weaken your resolve to get help for your teen. Remember, the main problem in all the stages of recovery is your teen's chemical dependence and your reactions to it. The next section of this chapter outlines four tasks. Tackle them, and you'll be well on your way to gaining the control you seek and to helping your teen deal effectively with the primary problem—chemical dependence.

TASKS OF THE CRISIS CONTROL STAGE

When you look at the problems your teenager and you face during stage one, you realize how chaotic your life has become. Now you must gather enough energy to seek the aid of a qualified counselor or therapist to help move your teen toward treatment. This stage has four tasks:

- Crisis Identification—identifying the core problem your teen is experiencing
- Problem Assessment—determining the specific nature of your teen's problem
- Intervention—explaining to your chemically dependent child in a loving, non-threatening way how his or her behavior has hurt many people and offering your teen help
- Contracts—establishing acceptable behaviors and basic family rules that both parents and teen agree to

The following sections explain these tasks in detail.

Crisis Identification

The point of crisis identification is to identify the core problem your teen—and therefore your family—is experiencing. You should seek crisis identification in response to any crisis or problem incident involving your teen: for example, violence, suicidal behavior, stealing, failing at school. When you meet with the therapist, you'll work together to unite the family so that members can deal with the specific or core problem at hand, for example, your teen's cutting classes at school.

It's very likely that your teenager will resist taking part in a crisis identification meeting. One way of getting your teen to take part is to appeal to his or her sense of integrity. Say, for instance, "You'll have a chance to tell your side of the story." If this doesn't work, try to make your teen believe that he or she may lose influence in the family: "If you don't take part, then we'll be forced to make some decisions about your future without you."

When you meet, be as clear as possible about your reasons for seeking help and about your goals for your teen. At the same time, realize that your reasons for seeking help might change as the therapist gathers more information about your family. For instance, after a few meetings with the therapist to settle the crisis of your daughter's cutting classes at school, you may discover that the real reason (the core problem) for skipping classes is alcohol or other drug use. This discovery will change your reasons for meeting and your goals for your child.

Of course, deep down you may already feel that your teen has a problem with alcohol or other drugs but you don't have enough information to know for sure. Luckily, with crisis identification, you don't need to know for sure. The therapist can help determine whether chemical use is playing a role in the crisis by asking whether your teen exhibits certain behaviors that may indicate chemical dependence.

Once you've described the problem as best you can, your next step in crisis identification is to agree not to change your child's behavior. Instead, agree to test his or her willingness and ability to help solve the problem and to accept a consequence.

To demonstrate how this works, let's return to the example of your daughter's cutting classes at school. To test her ability to be responsible for attending classes, you could ask her to agree to having a parent accompany her to school and to being restricted to the house after school for a period of two weeks. Agree that if she passes the test you'll acknowledge her responsible behavior by lifting the restriction. Likewise, agree that if your daughter fails the test, she'll have to bear a consequence for her irresponsibility—for example, being grounded on weekends.

This test brings two results. First, it demonstrates that responsibility, maturity, and change help contribute to smooth and happy family life. Second, when alcohol or other drug use causes complications and the problems in your teen's life, the test reveals this chemical use as contributing to chaotic and unhappy family life.

Expect at least two or three crisis identification meetings to identify your teen's and family's core problem. Once it's been identified, you may move on to the next task of Crisis Control, where you'll assess the problem in depth.

Problem Assessment

After parents identify the problem of chemical dependence through crisis identification meetings, they're often tempted to hurry up and try to carry out treatment without assessing the seriousness of their teenager's chemical use. Resist this temptation. Instead, take time to evaluate the problem fully before moving on.

With many teenagers, you may not have enough information to know *for sure* whether there really is chemical use or dependence. Meeting with a therapist for problem assessment will give you the opportunity and time you need to ascertain if chemical dependence is, in fact, the core problem. While the assessment is going on, continue to be a responsible and consistent parent, acknowledging your teen's mature behavior and enforcing consequences for irresponsible behavior.

Some of you may wish to hasten the assessment process because of pressure you're feeling from relatives, the school, the courts, or well-meaning folks who urge you to look for fast and easy answers. Your therapist can help run interference for you by speaking to those who are pressuring you. The therapist will also help you stay as calm as possible. Remember that you are where you are because your teenager is in trouble, and you can't expect a troubled teen to come right out and quickly and honestly state what's really going on. Assessing a problem takes time. Give it the time it needs.

During assessment sessions, teens will show a wide range of behaviors, including being withdrawn, charming, secretive, and even insulting and arrogant. Parents, too, may act in a variety of ways. You may feel embarrassed, hopeful, angry, or doubtful that the therapist can be of help. Parents tend to present opinions that are unsupported by hard facts, wishing that their teen's problem were still under their control.

Recognize that these behaviors—on the part of both teens and parents—mask real feelings. The teen may feel ashamed, knowing that he or she is failing miserably. Parents are demoralized and discouraged over how their child is turning out. Parents also often feel ashamed about their failure to control the present situation and feel angry both at their child and at each other for destroying their chance of family security. Likewise, parents generally feel profoundly sad and depressed. If they don't view the situation with despair, parents may look upon the therapist as some sort of therapeutic savior, the only person who understands their pain. When this happens, parents secretly expect a miraculous cure for their teen without doing any hard work.

What should you, as parents, expect? Expect neither too little nor too much. Instead, be realistic by keeping to the task at hand: assessing the problem. There are a number of steps you can take and people you can rely on to further the assessment process:

- Help with the assessment by gathering as much information from as many different people as possible about your teenager's behavior, especially as it relates to possible chemical use.
- Encourage your teen to agree to periodic but random drug urine testing conducted by qualified medical personnel.
- Talk to other parents who have gone through the same situation you're in to acquire more self-confidence and knowl-

edge about how to cope and manage in crisis situations. In self-help groups such as Al-Anon, Families Anonymous, and Tough Love, you can find others to help share your burden.

- Count on the social pressure from school, court, probation office, clergy, friends, and relatives. Their influence can help keep your child in the assessment process and will further treatment.
- Refuse to protect your teenager from the law if he or she commits a crime. People don't change their irresponsible behavior if it's not met with normal consequences. Too many parents have prevented the police from arresting their child, only to find themselves forced to have their child arrested later.

Some teenagers secretly reveal to a therapist that they have a problem with alcohol or other drugs. Some therapists disagree over whether they should break the teen's confidentiality and tell parents. Therapists usually try to keep a teenager's confidence. A therapist is often the first person the teenager has met with who can be trusted to help and not to judge or betray.

If the therapist believes that a youngster really wants to stop using and get his or her act together and is willing to take the necessary steps to do so, the therapist may well keep that person's confidentiality. At the same time, the therapist should encourage the teen to be honest with parents about his or her alcohol and other drug use.

If a teen is defiant or secretive but still takes part in assessment sessions, the therapist may well agree with the parents' suspicions regarding chemical dependence but encourage parents to keep working on the above steps. Experience has shown that when parents remain persistent, the truth will eventually come out.

However, you, as parents, by following the above steps, may determine that chemical dependence is most likely your teen's core problem. You may feel that you keep running into a brick wall as you strive to follow the assessment steps and help your teen. If so, it's time to bring some strong pressure to bear and to take on the task of intervention.

Intervention

If, in spite of all your efforts, you see that your child is clearly going "down the tubes" because of his or her use of alcohol or other drugs, you need to find a way to get your child into some kind of treatment quickly. An effective way to do this is called intervention. Vernon Johnson, founder of the Johnson Institute, pioneered the intervention process to help chemically dependent adults seek help, but the technique works equally well for teenagers.[3] Terence Gorski, a pioneer in the field of relapse recovery, says that intervention interrupts the vicious cycle of chemical use that is illustrated below:

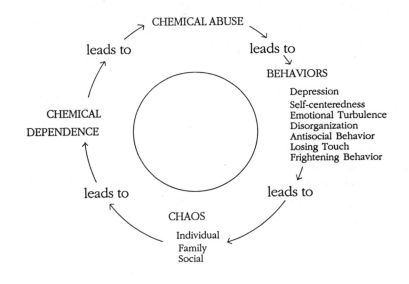

[3] For more information, read Vernon Johnson's *Intervention: How to Help Someone Who Doesn't Want Help: A Step-by-Step Guide for Families and Friends of Chemically Dependent Persons* (Minneapolis: Johnson Institute, 1986).

An intervention is a meeting involving the teenager who is chemically dependent, other concerned people, and a counselor or therapist who's trained in conducting interventions. Prior to the actual intervention, you, as parents, and other concerned people meet with the therapist to organize your thoughts and feelings and rehearse what you want to say. The intervention itself is carefully controlled by the professional therapist, who makes sure that it doesn't degenerate into a shouting match.

During this meeting, you tell your child in a loving, caring, and non-threatening way how it feels to be subjected to obnoxious, frightening, and dangerous behaviors caused by his or her chemical abuse. It's effective to use specific examples of their inappropriate behavior so your comments can't be ignored or denied as hearsay. You also let your child know that it hurts to see him or her suffering so much (failing in school, losing friends, being depressed, getting into trouble with the law). Before the meeting ends, you must be ready to present your child with a plan of action and a "bottom line." Your child must accept help and enter a treatment program that's ready to accept him or her. If your child refuses help and continues to use alcohol or other drugs, then you—as parents—must agree what additional "bottom line" steps you're prepared to take.

Some parents worry whether they should prepare for an intervention without their teen's approval. They fear that their teen will feel betrayed, hurt, or rejected. If you're feeling the same fear, consider the following:

- Your chemically dependent child is sick, in serious trouble, and desperately needs help.
- If you refuse an intervention, it's likely that your child will die prematurely as a direct or indirect result of his or her chemical dependence.
- If you do an intervention, it's likely that your entire family will get help to recover together.

If your teen becomes angry with you, recall that his or her anger is nothing new. This anger is just a sign of being ill. Intervention specialists reveal that most teens in this situation do feel angry. Nevertheless, teens also feel grateful that parents cared enough to make them get help.

Is there ever compromise in an intervention? Yes. Sometimes you may back off your first treatment choice in order to reach agreement. For example, rather than insisting that your teen enter a residential or hospital treatment program, you may agree that he or she will start treatment in an outpatient center. Such a compromise doesn't indicate that the intervention has failed. Just the opposite. You have, in fact, succeeded in getting your child into treatment. However, your teen might not stay chemical-free in your second choice of treatment. If so, place your child in the program that was your first choice.

Intervention is especially helpful in situations involving very defiant or avoidant teens and helpless families who believe "We've already tried everything." Very often, interventions enable the teen to hear—for the first time—the family say, "We love you, but it's time for you to let go of your pride and get help." Your child may finally realize that his or her chemical use has caused the family great distress.

Contracts

The last task of the Crisis Control Stage of recovery is the making of a contract. After an intervention at which a teen has agreed to get help through treatment, a contract made between parents and teen can be very helpful and successful. In the contract, parents and teen agree on acceptable behaviors and basic family rules, and also agree that treatment is a healthy step to take. The contract must fit the needs of the particular family and teenager.[4]

A contract must contain three important elements. First, everyone in the family must agree to very clear, specific behaviors that can't be misinterpreted. Second, there must be rewards for following the

---

[4] For more information on making contracts, read Dick Schaefer's *Choices & Consequences: What to Do When a Teenager Uses Alcohol/Drugs* (Minneapolis: Johnson Institute, 1987).

contract. This element is crucial because people won't easily change without encouragement and reinforcement. Finally, the contract must include specific consequences for misbehavior. (See page 22 for a sample contract.)

Contracts really work. A contract can help your teen realize how troublesome and painful his or her behavior is to you. It performs the important function of making your teen agree to specific and responsible behaviors. At the same time, a contract helps your family begin to unite around the idea of setting limits and to work together to help your troubled child.

Establish a contract with your teen and stick to it. Avoid you and your teen blaming each other for the family's troubles. Your whole family will then move out of chaos and crisis and move on to the stability and structure of the second stage of recovery.

ANSWERS TO QUESTIONS PARENTS ASK

Besides calling for help and asking "What should we do?" parents frequently ask the following questions of professionals.

Have I been too concerned over my personal wants and needs to spend enough time parenting my child? Somehow I've failed as a parent, haven't I?

Questions like these come right from the heart, and often from a broken heart. It's not easy for any parent to find a healthy balance between child raising and taking care of oneself. Many parents of chemically dependent adolescents have their own tough histories of pain and disappointment. Their own growing up may have included living with chemically dependent parents who were out of control and too deprived to pay enough attention to them. Put simply, those who taught them to parent couldn't teach them well. Like it or not, the responsibilities involved in guiding a chemically dependent child will take much of your energy and time that would otherwise go toward reaching your own personal needs, wants, and goals. But working hard to help your child recover will, in the long run, result in enough time, energy, love, and attention for everyone in the family.

I'm so angry I don't think I can ever forgive my child for what he's done to our family. What should I do?

You're asking this question from a state of chaos. You, your child, and your whole family are in turmoil. Things are pretty hot at this stage. Take time to cool down. An important parental task of recovery is learning how to relax, calm down, and keep a sense of humor and perspective so you can solve your problem. All of us have a point at which we get too hot under the collar or too self-righteous for our own good. It's difficult to calm down and admit when we've been acting foolishly. Unfortunately, this sort of behavior doesn't send our teen the message we intend to send. Instead of saying, "Look how your behavior has hurt me and the family," it says, "When you feel angry or agitated, it's okay to act like this."

It takes real strength to express anger appropriately, especially when you feel like screaming. But building such strength leads to forgiveness and the hope that family life will improve. So when you feel yourself getting bent out of shape in recovery, recognize that your anger belongs to you—it's no one else's fault—and that how you express it is your responsibility. Then resolve to find ways of handling your anger appropriately: take ten deep breaths; head out for some exercise; find a new hobby. Remind yourself that what you're doing is helping your teen learn how to handle his or her feelings maturely and that anger is simply one of those feelings.

Could my teen be having problems other than, or in addition to, chemical dependence that need professional attention?

This is a difficult question and one that chemical dependence professionals constantly discuss among themselves. Psychiatrists and psychologists with experience in evaluating and treating chemically dependent adolescents understand that adolescent mental disorders and chemical dependence can cause one another and can occur together. Psychiatrists are medically trained and can evaluate and prescribe therapies and medications. Psychologists can provide specific testing and counseling for emotional disorders but can't provide medication.

Remember, however, that chemical dependence is a life-threatening disease. If you suspect—or are sure—that your child is in this kind of trouble, it's best that you concentrate initially on the chemical dependence, because it's certainly endangering your child's life. Once your teen is free of chemicals, competent professionals can advise you how to deal with other problems that may show up.

Should we parents stop using alcohol or other drugs?

Generally, parents who use alcohol only casually ask this question. Parents who are dependent on alcohol or other drugs usually won't ask this question because they themselves are sick, and their denial and delusion prevent them from seeing that their own use of chemicals is causing them trouble. As a rule, I strongly recommend that all members of the family living in or visiting the home where the troubled teen resides agree to stop using alcohol—and other drugs, for that matter. The healthy modeling of parents and family members becomes a support to the troubled teen, who can't stop using or stay away from temptation on his or her own.

Some parents resist such abstinence, sometimes going so far as to insist that it's their *right* as adults to drink. Parents need to recall that using alcohol isn't a right but a privilege that our society grants to those of certain age. Parents can choose to forgo this privilege for the benefit of their child, and, ultimately, for their own benefit as well.

How do I choose a therapist? How will I know if a therapist is inept? Are there any warning signs?

Pick a therapist who (1) has a proven track record with this problem, (2) is recommended by reputable persons or groups such as Alcoholics Anonymous or Narcotics Anonymous, (3) listens well, (4) gives you insights that hit close to your heart and mind, (5) and, above all, is someone you respect and trust. A therapist should also be licensed by your state. He or she should have at least one of the following credentials: (1) certification in "addiction or chemical dependence counseling" or "addiction medicine," (2) several years of experience in treating chemically dependent children and families, (3) a degree from a university where training is provided in chemical dependence.

A word of caution: Beware the therapist or counselor who boasts of having all the answers, the best method of recovery, or the highest success rate. The problems you and your family are struggling to deal with are complicated ones. There are no simple answers. The decisions you make regarding your teenager's recovery take careful thinking and planning; they can't be made on the basis of simplistic answers or grandiose promises. Finally, the decisions are *yours* and your family's, not the therapist's.

What should I do if I think the therapist is too insistent on a set way to go about things or not objective enough to help my child and me?

Even the best of helpers can become too involved. Some may even lose control like members of your family and engage in argumentative, threatening, or petulant behaviors. If you see this problem developing, discuss it openly. If it continues, put a stop to it. You have enough problems. Good therapists go through years of training to keep their helping edge. Still, like you, therapists are human. Like you, they make mistakes. So don't be afraid to let your therapist know if you believe he or she has gone over the edge. Sharing this can lead to new understanding and even to a breakthrough in your child's and family's recovery.

Should I get a second opinion about my child's problem?

Keep in mind that the final decision about your child is yours. So a second opinion never hurts. As you discovered in this book's Introduction, it's very difficult to treat adolescents. A second opinion is especially helpful when you seem to be making no progress in the recovery process, when a new task makes you particularly uncomfortable, or when a therapist advises you to undertake a treatment program that might not fit your needs or the needs of your child.

Recognize, however, that some recommendations are exactly what you need but you may not want to hear them. A colleague makes this important point humorously: If you're walking down the street and someone calls you a horse, don't get upset. Just keep walking. If another person comes up and calls you a horse, consider it a coincidence and move on. But if a third person comes by and calls you a horse, get yourself a saddle.

So if you keep hearing the same opinion, it's probably sound.

SAMPLE CONTRACT

*This contract is for a teenage girl who has just
completed an intervention.*

I, Hannah, agree to the following:

I will attend *The New Way* outpatient chemical dependence program and will not miss a session for any reason. If I am sick, I will go to the session anyway, where I will be checked for illness. *The New Way* will excuse me from the session if it is determined that I am too ill to attend.

I will stay free of alcohol and other drugs and will agree to drug urine testing whenever requested by the program.

I will go right home after school and do my homework. My parents have the right to check my homework with my teachers.

On weekdays, my curfew will be 5:00 p.m. Bedtime will be 11:30 p.m.

On weekends, my curfew will be 11:00 p.m. Bedtime will be 12:30 a.m.

I will help at home with these chores: make my bed every day; take out the garbage on Mondays and Thursdays; set and clear the table for every evening meal.

I will not attend any parties unless a parent is present and has talked to my parents. I will go directly to and from the party.

My parents agree to provide me with an allowance of $___ for doing my chores each week. I will be docked $___ if I do not do my chores. If I lose all my allowance, I will not borrow money from anyone else. My father will give out the allowance every Saturday. If he forgets, he will give me an additional dollar.

My mother and I will spend time every Saturday out of the house doing something we both enjoy. We agree not to argue at all during that time.

I will follow these rules for one month from this day. If I do so, I will be allowed to extend my Saturday curfew by one-half hour.

If I continue to use alcohol or other drugs, I will immediately be placed in the following residential chemical treatment program:

_____.

If I get in trouble with the law, my parents will not protect me from the consequences.

This contract will be reviewed one month from today on the following date:_____.

Signed

Hannah _____

Father _____

Mother _____

Therapist_____

Date of Signing_____

Date of Review_____

CHAPTER 2

STAGE TWO: STABILITY AND STRUCTURE

At the second stage of recovery, the chemically dependent teen is receiving professional help. Your family begins to believe that there is a way out of its crisis, chaos, and pain. When parents and their teen can argue and come to an agreement with or without the help of an outsider (therapist), they find *stability*. Family problems will still exist, but angry words no longer push family members to explode into physical or verbal violence. Put simply, family members have learned how to shut up, sit tight, and listen to one another.

When family members agree to rules, appropriate behavior, and a daily schedule, they create *structure*. Working together, the family weaves a "safety net" under the recovering teen. This net of parents, siblings, relatives, friends, teachers, therapists, clergy, and others stretches wide to catch the recovering teen should he or she fall into relapse. The Stability and Structure Stage is generally completed in an inpatient or outpatient program—in a hospital, chemical dependence program, or residential facility.

As did Chapter 1, this chapter will look at the problems your teenager faces and the behaviors you might expect to see your teen exhibit during stage two of recovery. Then you, as parents, will learn about the problem behaviors that may show up in you and your family, and determine ways to deal with them. Next, the chapter describes three tasks your teen must accomplish during this stage. Finally, the chapter provides an outline of the different types of treatment programs that are available to help your teen. The chapter concludes by answering questions that parents often ask during the Stability and Structure Stage of recovery.

THE PROBLEMS YOUR TEENAGER FACES

For some time now, your teenager may have exhibited depression, self-centeredness, turbulence, disorganization, antisocial behavior, losing touch, and frightening behavior. Now that your teen is finally getting some help, you may have expected these behaviors to subside, but, for the most part, they haven't. You're struggling to figure out why your teen is acting this way. You wonder: "Is she just being stubborn and fighting the people who want to help?" or "Why is he still acting this way even though he's no longer using?" or "Is she suffering from some sort of emotional or medical problem?"

The problems your teenager is facing in stage two of recovery are difficult to describe. They involve many and varied emotions, wants, and needs. To get a better understanding of your child, here's what a typical teenager thinks at this stage:

> *When you first put me in this program, I really hated you for taking away my freedom. But you left me no other choice. I had to stay and get help. So, okay, I'll stay, but don't think I'll ever give you the satisfaction of knowing that I need your help.*
>
> *When I got here, I was a mess. I wanted to use drugs every day. My dreams were filled with getting high on pot, beer, coke—you name it. Sometimes it was so bad I felt like exploding and blowing off the*

*whole deal. So I gave the treatment staff here a whole
load of trouble. I knew I looked like a fool, but I didn't
care. I tried to look even more miserable so you'd feel
sorry for me and take me home.*

*I didn't know who I was, but I couldn't let you know
how ashamed I felt about what I'd done to myself and
to you. I mean, like how could you ever love me if you
knew? But I was really ticked off at you. I mean, you
were hypocrites, too. Every time I really needed you to
be strong or give me some limits, you acted like jerks,
like you were God or something.*

*I was screwed up, you know? It was like my head
couldn't put things together. Sometimes, I still can't
remember things. After being here awhile, and when
the drugs got out of me, I started to feel a little better. And
then these idiot counselors started bugging me to open
up. I didn't have a clue how I felt. So I just told them what
I figured they wanted to hear. In fact, I told them more.
You know, like I said that I did a lot more drugs and
booze than I really did. I wanted them and the other
kids here to think I was the toughest druggie around.
Actually—though you probably won't believe me—
what I told you about my drug use was the truth.*

*Later on, I started to feel lousy and ashamed, like I
was being forgiven for some big deal sin or something.
I needed to get out of here. I started to go along with all
the stupid program rules, figuring maybe the staff
would lighten up and let me leave.*

*Well, that's not the whole truth. I also followed those
dumb rules to make things better. But I'll tell you
something. I still don't know who I really am. All I know
is that I don't want to be a druggie any more.*

*Today they told me I'm getting out tomorrow. Yes!!!
I'll be glad to get out of here. I want to go home, but I'm*

scared, too. Like, I know that I'm powerless when it comes to alcohol and other drugs. I know I need to lean on you and my friends to stay sober and straight. One minute I'm afraid to go back to school and face everybody. The next minute I say, "But, that's their problem."
As I get ready to leave, I know I've got a lot of rules to follow, and I'm scared I might not know what to do when I've got a problem. I've got this recovery plan, and I'm going to try hard to stick with it. I want to make it.

I want to make it better between us, too. You know, get to know you all over again. So just be cool, okay? Don't get me mad by babying me or by pushing too hard. Like I said, I want to stay straight, but believe me when I tell you I still sometimes think I can use again. And, oh yeah, don't think I'll ever tell you any of this.

If you found these teenage thoughts confusing, you're not alone. Expect to be disoriented by the contradictions, insecurity, hope, wishful thinking, defiance, compliance, and confusion expressed by your teen. Your adolescent is going through a very perplexing stage on the way to becoming a more stable person and having some structure in his or her life.

BEHAVIORS TO EXPECT FROM YOUR TEENAGER

While your teen is receiving treatment, remember the old dictum "Actions speak louder than words." Too often parents vacillate between hope and despair as they listen to the confused words their child says during treatment. It's much better to observe the behaviors of your teen; how he or she acts will make it much easier for you to determine whether he or she is really committed to getting help.

As we've seen above, the problems teens face in the Stability and Structure Stage of recovery are difficult to pin down. The behaviors they exhibit, however, are a bit easier to predict. Generally, adolescents move through three phases of behavior while in treatment:

- Defiance
- Compliance
- Acceptance

In each phase the typical chemically dependent teen will exhibit both active and passive behaviors. For example, he or she might express anger openly or actively by yelling or shouting, or passively by not showing up for a meal or by slamming the door.

To illustrate these phases and behaviors, examine the case of a hypothetical teen we'll call Valerie. Valerie's mother brought her into a hospital chemical dependence program after Valerie—over a period of time—had miscarried, had been suspended from school for assaulting a classmate, had stolen some money, and had been violently sick at home because of an overdose of cocaine and alcohol. As her mother turns to leave her with the hospital staff, Valerie turns to her mother with tears in her eyes and cries pitifully, "Mom, why are you doing this to me? What did I do?" Valerie's mom feels like crying but walks away. She loves her daughter but also feels like killing Valerie with her bare hands and figures that no court in the land would convict her.

You can expect a child such as Valerie to move through all three phases of behavior listed above as she tries to come to terms with the help being offered to her.

Defiance. Valerie can't manipulate the hospital staff and most of her peers with her pleas for sympathy. So she agrees in words to follow the program's rules. However, she consistently breaks them, saying, "I forgot. It's hard to remember them all." Such behavior is called *passive* defiance.

Valerie isn't stupid; she knows what the rules are. She just won't follow them because, as she says, "I'm angry with my mom for taking away my freedom." As time passes, Valerie refuses to let go of her anger, allowing it instead to build up inside her. Valerie feels ashamed and helpless to change herself.

At this point, Valerie turns to *active* defiance. She confronts the treatment staff: "Screw all your rules!" She does her level best to break every rule she can. When that fails, she finds ways to be placed in seclusion, all the while crying and screaming as if she were being tortured. Sadly, Valerie's suffering is self-inflicted and is caused by all the emotional pain she's holding inside herself.

Unable to deal with this pain for long, eventually she opens up to a counselor who, in Valerie's eyes, seems to accept her even when she's being obnoxious. Valerie starts to settle down and settle in. Still, she's harboring thoughts of making her great escape from the hospital or of scoring some drugs.

Compliance. Soon Valerie figures out that "escape" isn't a great possibility, so she settles into *passive*compliance. She follows rules and attends group sessions regularly, but says little about herself other than remarks like "I just can't seem to get in touch with my feelings." She hopes her parents will grow tired of all the time it takes to go through the program and will let her come home. She sits back and waits. When this doesn't pay off, Valerie decides to take a new tack—*active* compliance.

Valerie figures that she can get discharged from the program if she pretends to want help. She puts on an Academy Award-winning performance, playing the parts of the "good patient" and the "good girl." Her peers in the program choose her as president of the unit. In group, she brings up personal issues and becomes recognized as a positive influence on others. She goes so far as to try to make up with her mom. She does all she can to make everyone think that the key to happiness is "participating in treatment."

During the active compliance phase, parents—and sometimes professionals—mistakenly believe that teens like Valerie are ready to get their acts together and live cooperatively at home. Too often parents miss, deny, or minimize signs that all isn't well. A part of Valerie really does want help. However, experience shows that during this behavior phase, nothing and no one can convince a teen such as Valerie that life will be any better without alcohol or other drugs. As we'll see below, this proves quite true in Valerie's case.

After having worn the cloak of compliance for awhile, Valerie becomes impatient with program peers who are more defiant. She tries to assert her independence from the group: "I don't need you to stay sober and straight. I don't need anyone. I can do it myself." Feeling frustrated, Valerie secretly breaks a major rule when she's found one night in the room of a boy who's also in the program. This action isn't simply a case of her acting like a typical teen who longs for a relationship. Rather, the professional clinician recognizes Valerie's action as her way of masking her depression, low self-esteem, and drug use. She has latched onto the boy as if he were a drug.

No matter Valerie's seeming compliance, she still can't let go of her druggie life-style and her need for thrills. Hopefully, she'll get help to see her actions for what they really are, and she'll confess how frightened and angry her problems make her feel.

This isn't to say, however, that all of Valerie's active compliance behavior has been worthless. No matter her intent or lack of contentment, she's trying on new and healthy behavior. She's acting "as if" she were healthy. Acting "as if" is a necessary step for teenagers in recovery: They have to try it before they buy it.

Acceptance. Valerie slowly progresses into passive acceptance. Although still afraid, with staff help she risks sharing her innermost thoughts and feelings. She doesn't want to be considered the leader of her peers. She's feeling depressed, because she's beginning to see that her former life-style and behavior were phony. Likewise, Valerie is really feeling the pain of how much she's hurt her mother.

This is an awkward time for Valerie. She's starting to act genuinely with others and has a positive identity, but she doesn't have enough experience to be confident about either. She knows that she has to give up her negative image and her destructive peer group, but she also feels nervous about taking such risks.

After more risk taking and finding peers who are sober and supportive, Valerie starts to blossom into *active* acceptance. She's on her way to the consistency and balance of the third recovery stage.

THE PROBLEMS PARENTS FACE

Parents of teenagers like Valerie will also face problems during the Stability and Structure Stage of recovery. Once you get professional help for your child, you'll experience a combination of feelings, including the following:

- *relief* that someone else will now watch over your child and share your burden
- *impatience* that no one is feeling a lot happier or safer right away; that the therapist helping your teen doesn't always have an easy answer
- *guilt* that maybe you played a role in causing problems in the family
- *shame* that your family is struggling and that others now know it
- *anger* at how your teen has treated you and at how much his or her chemical dependence has cost you emotionally, intellectually, socially, spiritually, and financially
- *fear* of the future, of another explosive crisis, of your child's rejecting you because you placed him or her into treatment
- *sadness* that your family life seems like such a failure and that your dreams of a happy and contented family may never be realized
- *loneliness* as if no one else can possibly understand your pain or help you to parent; as if your marriage or closest relationships can't support you in your pain
- *helplessness* and *worthlessness* because you've tried to make life better for your family and yourself, yet you see only failure
- *worry* that only the worst will happen in the future

What are you to do with all of these intense feelings?

First of all, admit that you have these feelings and that you're only human. Denying *your* feelings can make your teen feel helpless to deal with them, too, and with *his* or *her* feelings. Your child needs to see *you* being open. Your inspiration can help him or her stop defiant or resistant behavior. Although it sounds paradoxical, when you admit what you feel and let yourself feel—no matter how much it may hurt—you'll also feel relief.

Second, find ways to express your feelings without everyone exploding. Make sure that when you express them, you do so constructively and without blaming. For example, if you feel that your child isn't making as much progress as you had hoped or expected, don't automatically point the finger at the treatment program, therapist, or your child. Instead you may want to tell them in a calm manner how *you* feel—impatient and powerless. Own your feelings without projecting them onto others. Over time, you'll discover that your feelings will no longer be so frightening.

Third, do your very best to attend all the educational and therapeutic meetings available to you while your teen's in treatment. They'll help you better understand your feelings. Likewise, be aware that there are a number of books and pamphlets on enabling, co-dependence, family recovery, and so on that offer insights and solutions (see page 129 for a list of resources).

Finally, draw some support from the various self-help groups designed to help people who have a chemically dependent family member or loved one. Attend Al-Anon, Families Anonymous, and Tough Love group meetings. There you'll learn you're not alone.

Behaviors to Expect from Yourself and Your Family

Just as chemically dependent teens exhibit some problem behaviors at the beginning of the Stability and Structure Stage of recovery, you and your family will also exhibit certain predictable behaviors:

- Wanting yet fearing the help of professionals
- Enabling your chemically dependent teen
- Refusing to separate from your chemically dependent teen
- Refusing to detach from your teen's chemical dependence.

In what follows you'll learn about each of these behaviors and what you can do when confronted by them.

Wanting yet Fearing the Help of Professionals. The child you love and trusted has hurt, betrayed, and embarrassed you. You want help for him or her and for yourself, and you want to depend on the therapist to provide that help. At the same time, however, you feel fearful, unsure, mistrusting. You wonder, "If my own child could betray me, couldn't this stranger do the same?"

What Can You Do? Do your best to let the therapist know about your mixed feelings. Don't worry. The therapist won't be shocked! You want help, but you don't know what type of help you need. Good therapists understand that. Let the therapist know that he or she needs to be patient with you so you can be patient, too.

Enabling Your Chemically Dependent Teen. In normal usage the term "enabling" has a positive connotation: encouraging or sustaining someone or something. In the field of chemical dependence, however, "enabling" means something much different: encouraging or sustaining something that's harmful. Thus, enabling means unwittingly acting in a way that encourages or sustains a person's chemical dependence and irresponsible and self-destructive behavior. Far too often families enable a teen to remain chemically dependent by excusing, denying, or minimizing his or her behavior. It's important to point out that enablers usually mean well—they sincerely believe they're helping a chemically dependent teen by covering up for him when he misses work. Enabling is good intentions with bad results.

For instance, let's say that Valerie's mom accuses the treatment staff of being cruel because they've restricted family visitation in view of Valerie's repeated rule infractions. By attempting to waive the staff's restriction and visit her daughter, Valerie's mom may think that she's only trying to protect her child. In fact, she's teaching her daughter that antisocial and destructive behaviors—which precipitated the visitation restriction—are normal and healthy ones. Unknowingly, Valerie's mom is enabling her daughter's chemically dependent behavior.

What Can You Do? First of all, don't feel guilty about enabling. It's human. However, *be aware* of this tendency. Ask people you respect if they ever see you enabling your child. Like the parents of any teenager, you need friends to support you through these trying years. Second, read about enabling and attend meetings (of Al-Anon, Families Anonymous, for example) where other parents, relatives, and friends of chemically dependent people share stories of their successes and failures. Finally, get used to being unpopular with your child when you set a reasonable limit.

Refusing to Separate from Your Chemically Dependent Teen. We call the process in which a child and parent grow away from each other *separation.* In a healthy family, as children grow and mature, parents want those children to separate from them, and in fact such separation takes place as a matter of course. Not so in chemically dependent families. Consider the following example:

> *For a long time Julienne has resented her dad for working too hard and not being around when she needed him. She wants her dad to take more interest in her and to encourage her to succeed in school. He in turn would like to be closer to his daughter, but because he doesn't know how, he's convinced himself that raising a girl should be left to her mom and has abdicated his parenting responsibilities.*
>
> *Julienne has used alcohol, cocaine, and LSD heavily for three years and can't see that her use and hanging around drug dealers could lead to a tragic end. Now that Julienne is getting help, the professionals working with her recommend that she undertake a longer-term chemical dependence treatment program. This doesn't sit well with Julienne, who runs away. Her flight doesn't last long. The police pick her up and bring her home. Against the mom's wishes, Julienne's dad decides that now that she's home, that's where she should stay. He rejects the advice of the helping professionals, who argue that Julienne doesn't have a well-formed recovery plan and doesn't stand much of a chance of staying off alcohol and other drugs. He closes his ears to their*

*warnings, stating that no one has really ever given his
daughter a chance, but that he means to give her one
now.*

What we have here is but one example of the difficulties parents of chemically dependent teens have in separating from their children. Julienne's dad is having a lot of trouble dealing with the pain of separating from his daughter. He feels he must first get close to her before he can let her separate from him and become independent. If Julienne's dad removes her from the help she's getting, he reasons that he'll be the helper for his daughter, grow closer to her, and avoid separation. Going along with him, Julienne wins back both her dad and her drugs.

What Can You Do? First, realize that this stage of recovery gives both teens and parents the time to figure out (1) how to feel close and supported, (2) how to separate and become independent, and (3) how to stop worrying about losing one another's affection forever. With patience and hard work, families can find a healthy balance.

Second, examine areas of your own life where you may fear growing. Are you holding back in your work, from meeting new people, from dealing with a person who has long abused you? As you continue to grow and take healthy risks, your teen will benefit from your example.

Finally, examine whether you have any unresolved problems in separating from (or attaching to) your own parents. Find a suitable balance between being your parents' child and being an independent adult.

Refusing to Detach from Your Teen's Chemical Dependence. Teens who continue to deny their chemical dependence often try to involve their parents in a nasty little game. This is how the game is played: The teen gets to lie, steal, run away, use alcohol or other drugs, have sex promiscuously, and generally avoid any and all responsibilities. The parents get to chase, capture, rescue, and punish the teen. Engaging in this sad and tiring power struggle results in no one's having the time and energy to focus on a real and basic problem, the teen's chemical dependence.

Please don't misunderstand the idea of *detachment*. Detaching yourself from your child's chemical dependence doesn't mean that you should carelessly ignore his or her inappropriate behavior. Rather, it means being responsible *to* your teen, not being responsible *for* him or her. Your child's chemical dependence and chemically dependent behavior is your child's responsibility, not yours. Allow your child to shoulder it.

What Can You Do? When a recovering teen acts defiantly or bends rules, parents must learn to *detach* themselves from his or her chemically dependent behavior. You're learning to detach when you:

- become aware of the problem feelings you're experiencing
- don't panic
- realize that there's nothing you can do to force your teen to act responsibly
- recognize that the burden is on your teen to grow up and face his or her chemical dependence
- see that you can wait out any behavior and that with help your teen will eventually settle down

As you learn to detach yourself from your child's chemical dependence and its accompanying behaviors, you'll feel calmer, more in control, and you'll realize that you're an essential part of the team that's helping your youngster. At the same time, you'll see that your teen will also become more composed.

The most effective way for you to detach is to set up a program of clear, appropriate, and enforceable rules accompanied by effective consequences to help you deal with your teen's future behavior.

To ensure that rules are clear, both parents need to agree on them before presenting them to the adolescent. The easiest way to do this is to write down the rules, come to an agreement over them yourselves, then present and discuss them with your teen. In your discussion, you can deal with misunderstandings and clarify the rules together. For example, "Bedtime on school nights is 10:30 p.m." might be unclear;

instead, indicate either "getting ready for bed" or "being in bed." After you discuss bedtime with your teen, this rule might be rewritten and clarified: "On school nights, be in bed with lights out by 10:30 p.m." It's a good idea to post the rules in a place that's accessible both to you and to your teen.

Rules are appropriate when they reflect your teen's particular needs and abilities. When considering the appropriateness of rules, take into account (1) your teen's age; (2) your teen's fundamental needs; (3) the trust your teen has earned. Age is important because what may be appropriate for an older adolescent may not be right for a younger one: for example, a curfew time. Even though your teen may be suffering from chemical dependence, he or she still has some fundamental needs: privacy, friendship, independence, work, and the chance to take sensible and healthy risks. A rule that would restrict your teen's ability to have any friends would be inappropriate. Finally, although you certainly love your child, make rules based on the trust he or she has earned from you. Trust needs to be earned through responsible action; love is a given. As trust grows, rules can change. Remember, however, that for your chemically dependent teen, there's one rule that can't—must not—change: *There must be absolutely NO use of alcohol or other drugs.*

After you've established clear rules, be sure to enforce them. First, begin with yourself by modeling personal respect for rules. If your teen sees that you casually break rules, it will be very difficult for him or her not to do the same. Second, check whether rules are being observed. If, for example, one of the rules is a 12:00 a.m. weekend curfew, but your teen knows that you're in bed by 10:00 p.m. and never check what time he or she comes home, the rule is, in fact, unenforceable. Your job here isn't to police your teen, but to let your teen know, by your occasional checking, that you take the rule seriously. Finally, follow up infractions and compliance with specific and effective consequences.

Effective consequences need to accompany rules in order to help your teen experience the full effect of his or her behavior. First of all, to be effective, consequences must be set up and clearly understood in advance.

Second, they must be related to the incident at hand: "You took the car without permission; you'll be restricted in using it." Restricting car use when a teen breaks a rule about using foul language would be a consequence *unrelated* to the incident.

Third, consequences must be reasonable: "Starting today, you may not use the car for one week." It's okay if the consequence exceeds the violation. This shows the teen that the rule is important. It would be unreasonable, however, to demand that your teen turn over to you his or her driver's license for an indefinite period.

Fourth, consequences should be timely. Never wait to apply a consequence and never extend one into the future: for example, "Starting *next month*, you may not use the car for a week."

Fifth, consequences can increase in impact. If a teen continues to violate rules, the consequences for such violations can grow. This will help your teen realize that patterns of behavior are more important than isolated behaviors.

Sixth, consequences should be applied consistently, respectfully, and without ill will. No matter how good your system of rules may be, if you aren't consistent in the way you apply consequences, it will fall apart. Consistency provides your teen predictability and a much-needed sense of security. Likewise, the manner in which you apply consequences is all important. Consequences must be signs of your respect and care for your youngster, not weapons of revenge.

Seventh, remember that consequences apply not only to the breaking of rules, but also to complying with them. If your teen works hard to follow rules and is being responsible about recovery, be sure to have consequent rewards for such behavior: Extend curfews or bedtimes; grant more leniency as regards car use; plan to allow your teen to engage in an activity he or she especially enjoys.

Establishing a set of clear, appropriate, and enforceable rules accompanied by effective consequences allows you to detach yourself from your child's chemical dependence. More than that, by providing your family with healthy ways to deal with your teen's behavior in the future, it ensures that you will remain detached.

TASKS OF THE TEEN DURING THE STABILITY AND STRUCTURE STAGE

The chemically dependent teenager faces three tasks during this stage of recovery:

1. Detoxify and withdraw from alcohol and other drugs
2. Become aware of his or her powerlessness and inability to manage his or her life
3. Create a recovery plan

In the sections below, we'll describe each task in detail.

Task One: Detoxifying and Withdrawing from Alcohol and Other Drugs

Put simply, "detoxification" means abstaining from alcohol or other drugs and allowing the body the time it needs to purge itself of their poisons. "Withdrawal" is a term used to describe the physical and psychological discomforts experienced by a chemically dependent person who has stopped using chemicals.

In different ways, alcohol and other drugs *physically* affect the body. These physical effects need time to wear off; the body needs time to repair itself. Sometimes, in order to bring about that repair, some type of medication may be necessary. The chemically dependent teen has increasingly and continually used chemicals just to feel normal. Thus, the teen's body has become used to the presence of the chemicals; the teen has become physically dependent on chemicals in order to function normally. At the same time, the chemically dependent teen is usually psychologically dependent on chemicals. Psychological dependence means a desire or craving for the effects produced by the chemicals. The chemically dependent teen wants the mood change and actively seeks it. Thus, in a sense, he or she is doubly dependent. Detoxification and withdrawal from the alcohol or other drugs and their effects, then, can bring the teen some very real physical and psychological discomforts: poor sleep, loss of appetite, nervousness, depression, rage.

To accomplish the first task of detoxification and withdrawal, most chemically dependent teens need the support of a program that helps them deal with these discomforts and with cravings and temptations to use again. Most programs help the teen cope by teaching ways to:

- reduce stress with exercise, relaxation, and problem solving
- deal with the physical and emotional reactions of chemical withdrawal
- handle the normal but irritating little "crises" of everyday life. (For example, if a chemically dependent teen's radio isn't working, it may take him or her a lot of effort to stay cool and not fly off the handle and smash it to bits.)

As the parents of a chemically dependent teen, you should be aware that the task of detoxification and withdrawal takes time (on average from one to three months). That can seem like a long time, but a person needs time to get rid of the drugs(s) in his or body and the fuzzy thinking that goes along with drug use. It's true that your child may be leaving the support of a formal program just as he or she is completing the task of detoxification and withdrawal. However, while your teen has been working on the first task, he or she has also been working on the second and third. Accomplishing them will enable your teen to gain more self-confidence and realize some recovery success.

Task Two: Becoming Aware of Powerlessness and Unmanageability

This second task is the First Step of Alcoholics Anonymous and Narcotics Anonymous: "We admitted that we were powerless over alcohol and other drugs—that our lives had become unmanageable." (See page 125 for a complete listing of the Twelve Steps.) Task two is central to changing unhealthy behavior. As we saw in Chapter 1, recovery from chemical dependence means that you must realize and admit that you're powerless and in a crisis situation that's beyond your control.

Whereas parents may have admitted their powerlessness in stage one, chemically dependent teens usually have a harder time accepting this idea at first. Most secretly believe that they can handle everything, will live forever, and will never really get hurt. It's difficult to reason with someone who denies any trouble, doesn't care much at all about preparing for adulthood, and will be in real danger of dying prematurely should his or her chemical dependence go unchecked and untreated. When you point out the sad and dangerous reality of chemical dependence to teens, most take it as a personal insult.

Why? Like everyone else, chemically dependent teens want to feel good about themselves, to feel competent, to have control over their lives, and to have proof that this is true. Chemically dependent teens have found that using alcohol and other drugs quickly satisfies these needs for self-esteem. The high they get from chemicals fools them into thinking they're powerful, successful, and in control.

Even so, somewhere in the brain of your chemically dependent teen is the secret realization that his or her "druggie life-style" is phony, empty, and unmanageable. As a parent, you have to believe that your child is simply too afraid to confess this secret to you but that he or she really does want help. Believe this even when your teen insults you, begs you to remove him or her from the treatment program, or curses you and proclaims, "I don't care."

When your teenager was a child, he or she learned from experience that your warning "Don't touch the fire, or you'll get burned" was true. Your teen needs to learn the truth once again—from experience. Your teen needs to find a way of becoming honest and admitting that his or her chemical use made life horrible and painful, that he or she has been playing with fire.

Below, you'll find two lists to help you monitor your child's progress in accomplishing the task of becoming aware of powerlessness and inability to manage his or her life. The first list will help you know what therapeutic work to expect of your teenager. The second list will tell you what therapies complete this work.

Specific Therapeutic Work the Teen Must Complete in Stage Two of Recovery

- Assessing his or her chemical dependence
- Completing workbooks and writing a personal chemical use history
- Understanding the First Step of Alcoholics Anonymous and other self-help groups ("We admitted that we were powerless over alcohol and other drugs— that our lives had become unmanageable")
- Learning about chemical dependence and about the effects of alcohol and other drugs on the body and mind
- Understanding how negative behaviors affect other people
- Understanding how the seven problem behaviors described in the Crisis Control Stage (depression, self-centeredness, turbulence, disorganization, antisocial behavior, losing touch, and frightening behavior) relate to chemical dependence
- Recognizing the need for treatment of chemical dependence
- Realizing that the "druggie" peer group is not functioning normally
- Recognizing that academic achievement is healthy
- Dealing with the long-term problems caused by alcohol and other drugs
- Realizing that other psychiatric problems can co-exist with being chemically dependent
- Recognizing feelings and expressing them appropriately
- Longing to be part of the family again
- Understanding what constitutes true independence and freedom

Where a Program Does This Therapeutic Work at Stage Two

- In chemical dependence educational groups
- In confrontation groups that help teens face problems rather than run away from them
- In Alcoholics Anonymous or Narcotics Anonymous self-help groups, study groups, and other meetings
- In social-skills groups where teens learn to communicate
- In physical-exercise sessions that help lower tension
- In relaxation-exercise sessions that teach teens how to calm down when agitated
- In therapy that helps teens face social, emotional, and family problems, and helps them create a recovery plan to cope with these problems in the future:
  — individual therapy: for talking privately about very sensitive problems and for overcoming any resistance to help
  — group therapy: for discussing and solving personal problems by getting help from a group of peers who have similar problems
  — individual family therapy: for agreeing on the real problems in the family, making amends to and reconciling with one another, and preparing the recovery plan
  — multiple family therapy: where families (usually three to eight of them) discuss and help one another find solutions to similar problems, support one another, and confront one another in a caring manner

In conclusion, although the task of becoming aware of powerlessness and inability to manage one's own life is the responsibility of your chemically dependent teen, you can be very instrumental in helping your child accomplish it. If you notice that your child's treatment program seems to be missing an element on the list, feel free to alert both the treatment professionals and your teen to this.

Task Three: Creating a Recovery Plan

Now your teenager is free of alcohol and other drugs and working hard to deal with withdrawal. He or she is facing the reality of an illness that needs ongoing care, of a new and sober life-style, and of a positive identity. To accomplish all this, your teen also needs to create a personal recovery plan.

Your teen needs your help because chemical dependence has affected your whole family. With so many tasks to be dealt with in recovery, your child still has problems with clear thinking and can't make a commitment to a plan he or she can't remember. Your help is crucial in fashioning the recovery plan. The plan will become a part of parents' "safety net." The plan will help your teen cope before falling apart and resuming alcohol or other drug use.

The Second and Third Steps of Alcoholics Anonymous speak of being ready and willing to accept, and then actually accepting, a power greater than oneself to help one return to health and sanity. The recovery plan functions as this "higher" or "greater" power to help your teen stay sane, sober, healthy, and out of trouble. With a recovery plan, your child can better cope with mood swings, upsets, craving for chemicals, and conflicts. Supported by the recovery plan, your child learns to control anxious feelings, find the support of others, and solve the problem of saying "no" to old drug-using friends. The recovery plan gives your teen hope of staying healthy.

The following items can serve as guidelines for devising such a plan:

1. Professional Helping or Treatment Program (see Chapter 6)
   - aftercare program
   - individual and group therapies
   - family therapy
2. Self-help
   - Alcoholics Anonymous and other self-help groups
     — specific meetings to attend
     — number of meetings each week
   - identify: (a) the three most likely or dangerous situations in which your teen could be tempted to use alcohol or other drugs again: (b) ways to avoid these situations (Sometimes AA members refer to a member's relapse into using alcohol or other drugs as a "slip." For example, a recovering alcoholic who drinks a beer is said to have had a slip. Thus, a dangerous situation is one that involves a place, a person, a time, or a thing that's liable to cause a chemically dependent person to "slip.")
   - identify three people whom your teen can call for help when in trouble
3. School
   - which school to attend
   - homework time
   - which teacher(s), guidance counselor, and other school staff will:
     — become part of the "safety net"
     — give progress reports to the family, therapist, or treatment program
     — participate in treatment planning meetings
     — contact the rest of the school ahead of time to allow for a smooth reentry

4. Family
   - rules of acceptable behavior
   - times to be with the family
   - chores
   - allowance (if applicable)
   - bedtime
   - use of the car
5. Friends
   - acceptable friends
   - unacceptable friends
6. Social Activities
   - acceptable activities
   - unacceptable activities (dangerous situations or places)
   - curfew
7. A System of Stress Reduction
   - relaxation exercise
   - physical exercise
   - healthy nutrition
8. Relapses
   - consequences for using alcohol or other drugs
   - consequences for unacceptable behavior
9. Alcohol and Other Drugs
   - policy of adult use at home
   - complete abstinence
   - drug urine testing, if required
10. Privileges to be reinstated for Responsible Behavior
11. Coordinating the Recovery Plan—determine which professional will keep in touch with all members of the "safety net" to make sure that the recovery plan is followed (this person is called the "case manager")

Armed with a well-made recovery plan and supported by a "safety net" of caring people, your teen is well on the way to entering the third stage of recovery, Consistency and Balance.

ANSWERS TO QUESTIONS PARENTS ASK

The following questions are typical of ones that parents frequently ask professionals who are working with their teenager and family during the Structure and Stability Stage.

Why should my child be a patient in a treatment program? After all, those programs aren't like the real world. Why keep my teen from facing the hard knocks of life by protecting him or her in a program?

There's enough of the "real world" in a treatment program, but not the whole world. A program is designed to treat people with disabling problems, so that they can be restored to health.

In a treatment program, the chemically dependent teen can keep from falling apart completely. He or she finds a healthy way of living, explores feelings, learns about and understands chemical dependence, and tries out new behaviors without being laughed at or put down. Like the person who's suffering from heart disease, your child—who is suffering from the disease of chemical dependence—needs protection from and treatment for the disease. He or she also needs time to learn new skills in order to cope confidently and successfully with life.

But why can't my child by-pass all this program stuff and just go to a self-help group?

Unfortunately, most chemically dependent youngsters are too emotionally or physically disturbed, as well as too undisciplined to seek such help or participate regularly. Most adolescents don't have the tools to know how to stay sober and straight. Without help they can't learn how to accept and apply the principles of self-help groups such as Alcoholics Anonymous, Narcotics Anonymous, or Cocaine Anonymous. Treatment programs for adolescents, however, are designed to prepare teens to use self-help groups to their very best advantage.

Couldn't my child make it okay in an outpatient program? What's the big deal about inpatient? Does every chemically dependent teen need to be "put away" in an inpatient treatment program?
No, not every teenager. But, most do. Chemically dependent teens are very impulsive and have great difficulty in thinking before acting. Too many of their friends make alcohol and other drug use seem okay. Plus, your teen has many steps to master and life skills to learn as he or she recovers, all of which—experience has proven—more quickly and more easily in an inpatient treatment setting.

This isn't to say that an outpatient program for your child is totally out. Some teens have enough support and are serious enough about recovering to be treated in an outpatient program provided there is sound and supportive aftercare and follow-up counseling. However, some communities offer no or too few outpatient programs for adolescents, or the outpatient programs aren't structured enough for teenagers.

If inpatient programs are so important, why do most of them last only about thirty days?
At one time, there was some almost magical notion that a thirty-day program was all that was necessary to set a teenager well on the road to recovery. In fact, there's no sense at all to that program length.

Instead, communities need to be encouraged to support and build treatment programs that are geared not to fit a preselected number of days but to fit the specific stages of recovery.

Presently, hospitals provide the most expensive care, because they have to pay for more staff people to carry out recovery tasks in as brief a time as possible. It's true that any program needs more staff when it's providing for the *crisis control, stabilization,* and *structure* required by unruly adolescents in stages one and two of recovery. By the time teens are ready for stage three, they're *structured* and are able to *stabilize* themselves. Even though the teens need continued care, fewer staff need to be involved in that care. This would allow programs to run longer—as long as needed—and at the same time would lower treatment cost. Such treatment could be carried out in outpatient programs, longer-term residential programs, therapeutic school programs, and so on.

Sadly, the length of much chemical dependence care seems influenced strongly by insurance companies' and Medicaid's willingness (or unwillingness) to pay. Insurance companies and Medicaid seem to fear—mistakenly—that paying for such lengthier programs will cost more than a hospital stay. Thus, many will pay only for an expensive hospital stay, when a teen would do just as well in a less expensive, but longer and more appropriate, treatment setting, such as outpatient treatment, therapeutic group homes, therapeutic day schools, and residential centers. Unfortunately, we find many teens being readmitted to a hospital after relapsing because of the brevity of their initial stay. There, they start all over again.

Nowadays it's too expensive to keep anyone in a hospital after stage two. Sadly, many teens need a much longer program of treatment during stage two. Take the example of Jorge, who has been using crack cocaine, alcohol, PCP, and marijuana for the past three years. He experiences tremendous cravings for these drugs. He's also very depressed, experiences hallucinations, has cut his arms when agitated, and wishes to die. Jorge may need more than thirty days just to withdraw from drugs and feel more stable before he can take chemical dependence treatment seriously.

My youngster has other psychiatric problems. Which started first, chemical dependence, or the psychiatric problems?

It can be hard to tell. Adolescents are complicated and difficult to understand. The questions can only be answered over time and should be considered in the following order:

1. Before you rush to any conclusions, allow your teen three to six months of being off alcohol or other drugs. The use of these chemicals can mimic about every known emotional disorder and learning disability.

2. An adolescent is probably primarily chemically dependent if his or her family has a history of chemical dependence and if he or she resumes chemical use after a period of abstinence. Simply put, the child who comes from a family with a chemical dependence history is born with a brain that's less able to send a warning to stop when he or she is in trouble over chemical use. This teen needs special treatment to understand that he or she is powerless over chemicals and can't manage life while using them.

3. A chemically dependent teen will find and use any excuse, such as experiencing emotional distress from a psychiatric disorder, to use chemicals. He or she will mislead you into thinking that there's only an emotional problem but no chemical dependence.

4. If, after time, a psychiatric disorder in a teen doesn't disappear, then we're faced with an additional problem that will require special treatment. Studies show that at least 20 percent of chemically dependent people have long-lasting disorders such as major depression, personality disorders, eating disorders, attention deficit, learning disabilities, sexual and physical abuse, severe anxiety, and psychosis (being out of touch with reality). You may recall the term "dual diagnosis," which means being chemically dependent and also having other serious psychiatric problems. Some programs specialize in helping adolescents with dual diagnoses.

The psychiatrist wants to put my child on a psychiatric medication. But can't such medications lead to dependence, too? Why should you put a child on a medication when we're trying to teach him or her not to rely on any drugs to get through life?

If your child is receiving care for chemical dependence, it's normal for you to worry about this, especially if your child is in a psychiatric hospital. But keep in mind the following facts about psychiatric medications when they're appropriately prescribed and administered:

1. They keep symptoms, such as loss of sleep, appetite, concentration, and attention under control. They can also help control temper tantrums, overeating followed by forced vomiting, severe depressed

moods, and hallucinations. Psychiatric medications can help a teen who's suffering from symptoms so much that he or she can't ask for help, think clearly, or solve problems. Such medications are also helpful in treating very serious psychiatric illnesses. With the right medication, symptoms of such illnesses can decrease or disappear, allowing them to work on their problem with other chemicals.

Think of a psychiatric medication as acting like the volume control on a radio. If the radio is too loud, you can turn down the volume and still enjoy the music. Some chemically dependent teens are so disabled that everything in life sounds too loud. Without help they become agitated, rebellious, or else shut down emotionally. Medications lower this emotional intensity so that the emotional "music" isn't so intense. Then it's easier to listen and enjoy living.

2. Some people have permanent conditions that require medications over a lifetime. With adolescents, this can be difficult to determine. For most disorders, a teen should try being off the medication after no more than a year. Make sure to ask your doctor how long your teen should be on a medication.

3. Very recent research has revealed that some psychiatric medications can help cut down cravings for drugs such as cocaine and PCP.

Only a few psychiatric medications actually bring on chemical dependence. Anti-anxiety agents, such as Valium, can be used for life-threatening withdrawal from alcohol or sleeping pills. A doctor will prescribe these agents only for a short period in the hospital. Unlike adults, teens rarely experience severe withdrawal symptoms.

Stimulants such as Ritalin can also induce chemical dependence. At the same time, however, they can be of great help to children who have a true neurological attention deficit disorder. One of the most difficult problems professionals face is how to treat a chemically dependent youngster who has these severe attention deficits. Luckily, some agents can treat this condition without risking chemical dependence, such as anti-depressants, Clonidine, and Pemoline.

4. Teenagers don't become dependent on non-addictive medications. They do, however, worry about coping with life's challenges whether they're on or off them. They feel insulted to be told that they need something outside themselves in order to feel healthy. On the one hand, teens need help accepting that they can use these medications to cope better. On the other hand, teens also need to recognize that by using alcohol and other addictive drugs, they can't cope at all.

5. Just as some people get headache relief from aspirin while others do better on Tylenol or Motrin, so one psychiatric medication can provide better results than another in a particular person. If a medication's side effects are too strong, psychiatrists will discontinue the medicine, try another, or rethink your teen's problems and search for other solutions.

6. Medications are never a substitute for chemical dependence treatment and psychotherapy. Medications can't teach your child to be responsible or how to do hard, rewarding work. They can only make the going a bit smoother.

Everything about this program ticks me off. The treatment staff act as if they're all perfect and don't want to hear my opinions or complaints. After all, it's my child. I'm footing the bill. Why won't anyone listen to me?

If you're feeling angry about your child's treatment or are angry with one or more of the treatment staff, take a moment to determine where that anger is coming from. Do you feel that the staff has been making mistakes and that the last thing you need is another mistake? Or do you feel angry because the program keeps reminding you of personal problems when right now you're so exhausted you just want some rest? Or is your child on your case, trying to get out of the program, maybe trying to get back on drugs, trying to get you on his or her "side" and have the heat taken off the real problem—his or her chemical dependence?

Of course, knowing where your anger is coming from doesn't take it away. So now what should you do? First off, get back to basics. Cool down, get some support; exercise, don't eat too much, don't jump to conclusions. If you really believe the staff has made some mistakes, tell them so and let them know you want to work out a solution to this problem.

If you don't get satisfaction from talking to the program staff, don't give up. Ask to see the Program Director or the Administrator in charge of the facility until you can get things worked out. Even if your experience has taught you not to trust people, please accept that the treatment staff really does want to help. Good programs staffed by professional people listen to complaints, correct problems, and when wrong, apologize. Remember that to recover is to believe that human problems can be solved. Keep faith that great benefits can come from your willingness to work through your pain.

I think I'm doing all I can to make this treatment work, but my spouse [or ex-spouse] doesn't care. What can I do about it?

Although it won't be easy, first take the responsibility to stop any battling that may be going on between the two of you. Find some therapeutic help and—if necessary—some good legal advice that will protect your interests and bring peace. Be sure to tell the treatment staff if you have fears about any harm the other parent may be causing to your child's recovery (for example, his or her own chemical use). Then rely on the helping professionals to offer a variety of techniques to help get the other parent actively and helpfully involved. Your spouse or ex-spouse may need additional help for chemical dependence or for a psychiatric illness.

If this treatment is supposed to be for my child, why is the staff asking me all these questions about my life?

Anyone who lives or works with chemically dependent persons is affected by the disease. (Even therapists can burn out if they don't take care of themselves and ask for help when this difficult work seems overwhelming.) Like every other parent, you've had experiences that shape the way you raise your child. For example, growing up with a chemically dependent parent, suffering the death of a close family member, being the victim of neglect or abuse, or lacking knowledge about feelings can change your view of life. Seeing your child lose control can often uncover some old pain that you'd prefer to remain buried.

When someone asks you about your childhood or another part of your past, try to understand the questions without feeling threatened. Often, what the questioner is really saying is, "Tell me what personal healing you have to do. If you can heal and work to help your family, then you can give your chemically dependent teen hope of changing for the better, too."

CHAPTER 3

STAGE THREE: CONSISTENCY AND BALANCE

You will know that you've reached the third stage of recovery when you see that your teenager:

- very rarely has a serious crisis
- follows the recovery plan, doesn't disobey it, but will discuss with you how it should be changed
- still grumbles, mumbles, and complains how much he or she has to do in a day, but does it anyway
- accepts the consequences for breaking a rule, failing a test, breaking curfew, and so on
- doesn't get into any major trouble for a month after accepting a consequence
- can laugh with you or tell a joke
- acts responsibly at home: for example, does chores without being asked

- complains to you how his or her siblings should start behaving; "Otherwise you'll have another kid like me in treatment"

In other words, your once-defiant, wild, frightening, depressed, and aggressive teen is beginning to mature again before your eyes. Occasionally you'll hear an "It's not fair" or "You're such a jerk" or worse thrown at you. Let your teen know how you feel about such remarks but don't personalize it. Remember, many recovering family members are discovering that they can feel safe sharing their intimate feelings with each other, as well as laugh together and enjoy each other's company.

However, don't write "...and they lived happily ever after" to this story just yet. You, your chemically dependent teen, and your whole family are aiming for *consistency* (that is, "keeping on keeping on") and *balance* (managing all of life's demands with composure). Much work remains to be done.

The following sections explain this work. First, we'll examine the problems your teenager faces and the behaviors you might expect from him or her during stage three. Second, we'll look at the problems parents face. Third, we'll discover the tasks necessary for teens, and then for parents, to achieve and maintain consistency. Fourth, we'll describe the tasks teens and parents need to accomplish to achieve and maintain balance. We'll conclude the chapter by examining some typical questions that parents ask during the Consistency and Balance Stage of recovery.

THE PROBLEMS YOUR TEENAGER FACES

During this stage of recovery your child can still have strong withdrawal symptoms. Relapses, which will be discussed in detail in Chapter 5, can also occur. Know that in this stage your teen will have to face problems in the following areas:

- learning how to solve problems
- working on building a positive and healthy identity and then achieving it

- building confidence so he or she won't panic when a difficulty occurs
- learning how to handle the demands on his or her time that will be made by family, friends, work, and school
- beginning to believe that life is rewarding and that finding dangerous thrills won't satisfy deeply held needs, wants, or expectations

With time, patience, and hard work, your youngster can reach *consistency*. After that, life becomes a question of *balance*. Many competing forces will tug at your child, threatening to throw him or her off balance. However, as it becomes easier for your teen to solve everyday problems, he or she will possess the confidence and the motivation to spend time in activities other than treatment. Soon, involvement in sports, schoolwork, alcohol- and other drug-free parties, and other events will also be taking up his or her time.

If your teen complains a bit about the "problem" of balance in his or her life—about difficulties in handling all the different demands people and things are making—feel happy about it. Your teen is re-entering the real and normal world. Your once-upon-a-time wild child is developing a sense of who he or she really is. Stay optimistic as you help your teen face the normal demands of growing up. Help your teen realize that life's problems can be faced and solved, even if the solution isn't immediate. The more problems your teen solves and the more accomplishments he or she makes, the more self-esteem and confidence your teen acquires.

Behaviors to Expect from Your Teenager

As odd as it may seem, recovering adolescents sometimes feel scared when they realize they're acting in healthy ways. This fear is a kind of identity crisis in which the teen is saying: "Is this me doing this? It's hard to believe that I can do this well. I'm just afraid I won't be able to keep up the good work." Having become more self-aware, the recovering teen is suffering from the shock of having a positive identity. This recognition is so new and unfamiliar that the teen fears that it will last only as long as other "highs" have—namely, those induced by alcohol or other drugs. To prevent a relapse and get your teen through this crisis, you may need to offer assurances that acting in a healthy way has its own "high," its own reward, and that he will be able to continue to act more and more like this as recovery progresses.

Expect your teen to lose emotional control at times. He or she will challenge the recovery plan or "forget" about it now and then. For example, your teen might push curfew limits or "forget" to do household chores. (Don't forget that many teens with no chemical dependence problems exhibit the same "testing" or "forgetting" behavior.) During this stage of recovery, it's common to notice that your teen may still fear facing social situations, have a psychiatric disorder worsen, feel more stress, peer pressure, and be unable to talk about needs. Some youngsters will replace chemical dependence with other dependencies such as work, sex, fighting, sports, cars, food, risky situations, or even homework. Although some of these activities seem more appropriate than chemical dependence, teens too often get involved in them as a way of avoiding having to deal with conflicts, disturbing feelings, and the challenges of recovery.

Put simply, whenever the teen feels like giving up, he or she may revert to trying alcohol or other drugs again, thinking, "I'll do it just one more time to see if it was all that bad."

If your child exhibits any of these behaviors, including using chemicals again, don't give up on your hopes for recovery or lose confidence in your ability to supervise your youngster. Know, however, that although it's typical for teens to "test" limits, such behavior can have serious consequences for the recovering adolescent. So be on the watch for both minor and major problems that might erupt in the following areas:

Aggressive and Sexual Urges or Impulses. Bill slugs someone who calls him a wimp. Natasha is found partially clothed with a boy in the back seat of his car.

Friends. Jane sneaks telephone calls to her old druggie boyfriend. Malcolm stays home on weekends, alone, bored, and lonely.

Family. Bernardo refuses to go with the family on a picnic. Kim has a big argument with her parents about babysitting, chores, money, and freedom.

School. Margo doesn't show up at school one day. Quan fails an easy test.

Work. Katrina is fired after only one week on the job. Frank asks his parents to front him some gas money even though he's just gotten a paycheck from work.

Drug Use and Dangerous Situations. Steve is found with a friend who passed out in a car. Maria is hanging out at a mall where a lot of drug dealing occurs.

What do behaviors like these indicate? Do they mean that recovery is lost? Not at all. An adolescent really can be recovering yet still feel sorry that the thrills and quick, feel-good, chemical high are no longer possibilities. With that high unavailable, the teen may feel bored, a feeling that seems abnormal. Such a teen needs more experience with being able to do something healthy with the boredom. If the youngster doesn't know how to find some safe thrills and how to deal with boredom, relapse can happen.

The recovering adolescent must also learn to apply in the real world the life skills learned in his or her rehabilitation program—problem solving, identifying and coping with feelings, reducing stress, and refusal skills.[5]

THE PROBLEMS PARENTS FACE

No matter the type of professional help a chemically dependent teen is receiving, he or she generally returns to living with the family sometime during stage three of recovery. When their teen returns,

---

[5] For more information about how to help teenagers practice life skills, read *Parenting for Prevention* by David J. Wilmes (Minneapolis: Johnson Institute, 1988).

parents often find themselves faced with new or additional stresses: ongoing demands of treatment, new or old family conflicts, and especially the teen's mood swings and other disturbing behaviors. Everyone in the family seems more needy, and parents often feel it's their place to make everyone happy—an impossible job!—and feel guilty when they can't.

As parents, be assured that after a period of adjustment, your family will gain confidence in expressing feelings appropriately, living with conflicts and the occasional emotional upset, and solving everyday problems. When this happens you'll have reached *consistency.* You'll have more time to pay attention to activities other than those directly related to treatment.

This isn't to say that *consistency* will alleviate all problems. Nothing will do that. In fact, as your teen becomes more *balanced,* you may find that you're having a problem with balance yourselves: balancing your need or desire for family closeness with your teen's need for independence. As your child seeks independence, don't be surprised to find yourselves feeling nervous and worried or parenting with too much "tough love." You must work hard to recognize that your teen isn't falling back into old rebellious habits but is being consistent about his or her treatment and recovery and is striving hard to balance all the demands for his or her time.

At this stage of recovery, parents' marriages may also begin to show some signs of trouble. The chemically dependent teen is finally growing up and doesn't demand so much parental attention. Spouses, who now have time to concentrate on other things, may begin to notice some of their own unmet needs, forgotten dreams, abandoned goals. Sometimes the stress of their past dealings with their teen starts to take its toll on the mind and body. Spouses need to look to their own emotional and physical well-being, to find time to relax and heal.

TASKS NECESSARY TO ACHIEVE AND MAINTAIN CONSISTENCY
Normally, it can take from one to two years to see your chemically dependent teen acting consistently. If your child has emotional problems, it may take longer, because problems with emotions, learning, and attention can be very complicated or affect your child's ability to learn how to stay free of alcohol and other drugs.

The Teenager's Tasks

To reach *consistency*, the recovering adolescent needs to accomplish seven major tasks, summed up in the following resolutions and insights:

1. "I will learn to stay sober and healthy one day at a time." Early in the third stage of recovery most teens make a commitment to stay chemical free for more than one hour at a time. This is no small commitment. Every day, old friends and even strangers present the teen with temptations to use chemicals again. It's difficult for a young person to "just say no" when past experiences include a lot of getting high but very little standing up for personal well-being.

2. "I will learn to cope with problems of daily life without panicking." During the Great Depression of the 1930s Franklin Roosevelt cautioned Americans that "the only thing we have to fear is fear itself." President Roosevelt warned us that if we panicked when times were bad, we'd never get ourselves on the road to economic recovery. The same can be said of personal recovery. When overly fearful, nervous, or panicky, the teen is in too disturbed a state to solve everyday problems. That's why the recovering teen needs to learn constructive ways to handle life's difficulties.

3. "I have to think before acting so that I don't bring more problems on myself." Being consistent about one's behavior means knowing how to prevent oneself from creating additional problems. It can be difficult for the recovering teen to fight a sudden impulse to cut school, break a family rule, or give in to a sexual urge. The teen has to learn to stop and realize that giving in to impulsive behaviors

generally brings on even bigger problems. The teenager also has to believe that, with control, will come greater rewards and discovery of better things to do with his or her time.

4. "I can see a relapse coming on and prevent it from happening." (*Note*: Relapses will be discussed in detail in Chapter 5.) Recovering teens need to learn to recognize early warning sings that can lead to relapse. Because coping with stressful situations can precipitate a relapse, recovering teens need to know what immediate steps to take to avoid them. Otherwise, they may fall into old dependent behavior, pick up a new out-of-control behavior, or find a substitute dependence in order to deal with such potential "relapse situations."

5. "To like myself and feel better, I realize that I have to take responsibility for my other problems as well as chemical dependence." Eight out of ten chemically dependent teens may also have more than one other serious problem that requires treatment. Such problems include depression, suicidal thinking, extreme distrustfulness, uncontrollable rages, learning disabilities, eating disorders, a chemically dependent parent, physical or sexual abuse, and so on.

Consider how much time and patience it can take an adolescent to get over the shame of having lots of problems; become "sick and tired of being sick and tired"; admit to allowing one's self-will to run riot; recognize that it's time to face one's problems rather than use alcohol or other drugs to escape the resulting emotional pain; learn to tolerate hurtful feelings and find better ways to handle life's difficulties; and rely on others for support when times are tough. As you can see, consistent healthy living is no small task; it takes time, courage, and hard work.

6. "I can accept freedom from alcohol and other drugs as a way of life, but only one day at a time." Living "one day at a time" is important. To promise never to use alcohol or other drugs for the rest of one's life seems like an overwhelming task to your child. It's common for a recovering teen to say, "Maybe I should try using drugs later, just one more time, to see if I really can't control them." A statement like this speaks to most teens' need to keep their options open and never to promise an adult anything unless it feels real. If a chemically

dependent adolescent needs to experiment and "hang loose," deadly consequences can come from using alcohol and other drugs. So it makes sense—if you understand what teenagers are all about—that a promise to stay drug-free "one day at a time" is easier to make and more likely to be kept.

7. "To accomplish my recovery tasks and meet my goals, I need to rely on others to help me out." During this recovery stage, besides your help, your child should have the aid of a sponsor from a self-help group. Experience and maturity count. The sponsor should be at least 18 to 20 years old, be at least three years older than your teen, and have at least two to three years of continuous sobriety.

The Parents' Tasks

Like your chemically dependent youngster, you and the rest of your family have work to do to be *consistent*. Here are ten important tips to help you on your way:

1. You might find yourselves at times getting angry about the demands that treatment makes on your time and energy. Your chemically dependent teen may pressure you to abandon therapy. Your teen may protest, "Just let me go on with living. I don't need all this help anymore. I can do it alone." If this happens, know that your child hasn't yet begun to take seriously that he or she has to rely on others to stay drug-free (see the second and third steps of Alcoholics Anonymous and Narcotics Anonymous).

What can you do? First, don't give in to your teen. It's normal for teens to want to get out of a treatment setting. Know this and relax. Second, talk with your supports (for example, parents you trust who have gone through similar problems, therapists, clergy, or other teens in your child's program). They can help you see that this is not a big crisis and that your teen will eventually settle down and accept treatment.

2. Keep to the recovery plan. Review it whether things have been going better or going worse.

3.   By your example, teach your teenager to accept anxiety as part of and helpful for recovery. Feeling anxious can be your sign to stop avoiding a problem, start facing up to uncomfortable feelings and conflicts, and begin problem solving now.

4.   Stay alert for your child's urge to use alcohol or other drugs, especially when things are too good to be true or too bad to ignore.

5.   Stay consistently in touch with everyone involved in the "safety net," whether times are good or bad.

6.   Learn that it's normal to mistrust your teen during the recovery stage. Don't feel guilty. It will take time for you to get over all your heartache. If everyone's behavior remains consistent, your trust for each other will naturally grow.

7.   Keep a *balance* between limit setting and getting along together. This isn't the time to loosen up your rules and limits. Right now, your youngster is too fragile to take full responsibility for coming home at a vague "decent hour" or starting homework "sometime tonight." Your teen needs rules that are much more specific: "Be in the house at 10:00 p.m." and "Start your homework at 7:00 p.m. and finish before 10:00 p.m." Remember also to spend some time playing, working, and cooperating with your teen. Such positive times will make it easier for you to give, and for your teenager to take, a consequence for breaking a rule or limit.

8.   Generally, if you have to say something negative to your teen, find two positive things to say before you offer the negative. Families in recovery find it too easy to pick on faults and too hard to praise. Many studies have shown that if you want someone to change behavior, appreciation works better than ignoring or constantly criticizing. If you're thinking to yourself, "Yeah, but my kid never does *anything* good," remember that while that might have been the case during the first stage of recovery, Crisis Control Stage, he or she is now in the Consistency and Balance Stage, so there has to be *some* good behavior. Look closely, and you'll find it.

9.   As family members form stronger emotional bonds, the recovering teen begins feeling and behaving like a normal adolescent

with a positive personality. For this to happen, your teen needs you to be available to prove that relationships can be loving, respectful, and fun. Eventually, your child will feel hopeful and be motivated to grow up to be a successful human being.

10. Look for signs of emotional problems or chemical dependence in other family members. There's a basic principle about families living with a troubled child: As the child starts to get better, parents and siblings suddenly start to focus on and complain about their own unhappiness. Other hidden problems will suddenly appear. Don't be dismayed. Yes, you may have more work to do. Still, you're fortunate to have these problems out in the open where you can solve them—and you do have the skills to solve them!—instead of having them hidden and causing deeper problems.

TASKS NECESSARY TO ACHIEVE AND MAINTAIN BALANCE

It may take up to a year to accomplish the tasks necessary to achieve and maintain *balance*. Meanwhile, both the recovering teen and the family remain involved in their own recovery plan and participate in self-help groups. Both believe that there must be a solution to any problem and that they can eventually find it together. No one needs as much help as was required in the earliest stages of recovery, because now the family has grown in confidence and in its ability to solve problems.

The Teenager's Tasks

To achieve and maintain *balance*, the recovering teen must accomplish ten tasks. Put in a teenager's own positive words, these tasks are:

1. "I can learn how to balance the demands that my school, job, friends, parents, therapy, sponsor, and others make on me." Everyone in your teen's life has rules, needs, and time pressures, and everyone expects satisfaction. Your youngster has some difficult lessons to learn on the road to adulthood. One is listening to the needs of others with

a cool head while putting personal needs aside. Another is realizing that no one can please everyone. Check out the example of Juan:

Seventeen-year-old Juan must attend Alcoholics Anonymous meetings, attend school regularly, keep up with homework, and still find time to let his girlfriend Jenny know he's still crazy about her. One Saturday night Juan needs to see his grandfather who's in the hospital. Dad and Mom need him to drive his little brother to the Boys' Club. And his boss at the shoe store wants him to work late in order to finish the inventory check.

Juan—and other recovering teens like him—must learn to negotiate and balance these demands.

2. "I have to learn not to lose it when I doubt myself." Failures at school or work can happen. Relationships can break up. People may still accuse an innocent teen of wrongdoing, even after he or she has remained drug-free and has tried hard to shake a bad reputation. The challenge of new responsibilities at work, school, home, and in relationships can seem overwhelming to the recovering teen and cause him or her to have self-doubts. As parents, you can be helpful in reassuring your child: "You'll be okay. Life will go on. This stress is a part of life. It's just that now that you're drug-free, you're really experiencing it for the first time. Hang in there. Tomorrow *will* look brighter." Reinforce your support by posting an inspirational picture or poem (for example, "If," by Rudyard Kipling) in your teen's room. Offer a reassuring hug. If you feel you and your child need more support than you can give on your own, don't hesitate to encourage your son or daughter to talk to a friend or sponsor.

3. "I can plan so that I can prevent problems from happening and so that I can be more successful." Planning is an adult skill that involves problem solving, learning how to think before acting, and delaying personal gratification. Deferring satisfying immediate needs can often pay off in much larger rewards later on. Remember to allow your teen time to learn how to plan so that his or her confidence will grow.

4. "I have faith that I can keep myself together when I'm stressed out. I can still get support when I need it." This is also a major goal for preventing relapse (see Chapter 5).

5. "I know what I do to get myself in trouble. I don't have to hate myself for it." Knowing and admitting one's faults relates directly to the fourth and fifth steps of recovery found in most self-help groups. Step 4 requires the recovering person to make a "searching and fearless moral inventory," while Step 5 requires the person to admit to a higher power, oneself, and another person "the exact nature of...wrongs." Knowing and admitting one's faults is an essential part of recovery, as well as part of the maturation process. Mature adults usually know their weaknesses and can openly admit them. It's important for recovering teens to see this modeled by significant adults. When recovering teens can openly acknowledge their weaknesses, they're less likely to be hurt when reaching for a goal. Look at the example of Allie, a recovering sixteen-year-old:

> *Allie works in a restaurant. She wants to tell off her boss for not giving her a raise as he did for all the other kids who work with her. In the past, Allie would have gotten right into her boss's face, minced no words while telling him exactly what she thought of him, then stalked out. But now, Allie realizes that her old druggie behaviors like wanting immediate gratification and rewards, being insulting, and blowing her cool will never get her a raise. So Allie meets with her boss and expresses how hard she has worked and how disappointed she is at being passed over for a raise. She asks her boss for honest criticisms and suggestions for how to improve. In the end, whether or not Allie's boss grants her a raise right away, he'll realize that she has integrity and cares about her job. He'll know that Allie is the kind of employee he wants in his restaurant.*

6. "I keep *my* recovery plan alive and won't give it up." The recovery plan acts as a higher power to keep the teen moving in the

right direction. It's a life-saver and a life-giver. A balanced teenager realizes this and takes responsibility for his or her recovery plan.

7. "I know how to make things better if I'm bored, or if I need some thrills, or if I'm feeling lonely." Once on the road to recovery, the teen can find life getting dreary. Going to school or work, doing homework, and seeing old friends is still fulfilling, but teens still ask, "Is that all there is?" Recovering teens normally miss the excitement, thrills, and action that once came with chemical use, and it's understandable that they would still want these things. They do have to realize, though, that real excitement doesn't come from using chemicals and that one can't always get what one wants right away.

As parents, you must realize that alcohol or other drugs actually did make your child feel very alive, even though in truth these same chemicals hurt your child severely. Finding "legitimate thrills" will require some patience, hard work, and creativity on the part of your teen. Encourage your teen to stretch himself or herself by substituting challenges for thrills, real challenges that provide long-lasting satisfaction. Music, drama, dance, active sports, surfing, bike racing, and rafting are but a few of those challenging opportunities.

8. "I know when I'm getting too dependent on something, and I can stop myself." Recovering teens must learn to recognize and resist having addictions, those temptations that say, "Hey, here's an easy way out of your nervousness, depression, or anger." Failing to do so can lead to relapse.

9. "I know when I need a challenge in my life, because life is boring. I stop taking on challenges when life becomes overwhelming." The teen must recognize that keeping a balance involves pacing oneself. For example, in order to prevent stress—which can lead to relapse—a teen may have to choose a job that requires fewer hours than one held in the past.

10. "I am thinking of my future—I can think about learning a trade or going to college, leaving home, and being more independent." Many older adolescents in the later part of the Consistency and Balance Stage have to start becoming more independent and self-sufficient. Some, of

course, try to take on too much, while others fear to explore their future. The latter may still feel a bit shaky and need to depend on parents for emotional and financial support. Guidance counselors, therapists, vocational counselors, and clergy can help an older teen make the big move away from home.

The Parents' Tasks

Parents also have to achieve and maintain balance, both in their own lives and in their dealings with their recovering teen. To do this, parents need to deal with the following tasks:

- their parenting
- their eventual "empty nest"
- their marriage and other relationships
- their lingering resentments
- their involvement in support groups
- their personal problems

Parenting. Sometimes parents don't act flexibly enough to allow more freedom, because they fear losing their child. When you see your teen behaving predictably and responsibly, and when you notice how your own feelings of trust toward your teen have increased, it's time to lighten up, let go of your fear, and negotiate new rules and limits with your *consistent* and *balanced* teenager.

The Empty Nest. Eventually your child will leave the nest, and your parenting duties will cease, or at least diminish considerably. When that bittersweet time comes, you can shout "Hallelujah!" and shed a tear or two. But what about now?

Now you need to plan what you want to do with *your* life, especially if parenting has been your main career and you feel guilty about doing something for yourself. Anticipate experiencing some pain of separation and some loneliness. But remember that people never *totally* separate and that there's no bond deeper or stronger than that between a parent and a child. If you plan to handle the time of separation well—with compassion, patience, and grace—you'll lower the stress on yourself and on your child. You'll be ready to create a new relationship with your child and to discover a new life for yourself, one in which you can focus more attention on your marriage and other relationships.

Marriage and Other Relationships. Once teens reach and maintain balance in their recovery, it's not unusual for their parents to begin feeling that their relationship is a bit shaky. Now that most of parents' time and patience aren't focused solely on the recovering teen, many spouses discover that they have marital problems to solve or long-delayed needs and goals to fulfill. If you notice this in your relationship, take time to communicate, negotiate, plan. Perhaps you need to go away for a long weekend together or to take that second honeymoon. You may find yourselves arguing and feel that your spouse isn't being sensitive to your emotional, physical, spiritual, intellectual, or sexual needs. Remember, you've learned well how to exercise patience; exercise it with each other.

Lingering Resentments. After a year of more of working on recovery, your family is stronger and more secure. But if you notice that tension, mistrust, and fear still exist in your home, even though everyone is behaving well, you may be suffering the effects of some lingering resentments about your recovering teen's chemical dependence. For example, do you still think about how your chemically dependent son smashed up the car, was busted for drugs, and embarrassed you in front of the neighbors? Or do you still feel indignant about the way your daughter pulled a full-blown temper tantrum in front of all the relatives at Thanksgiving, ran out of the house calling you names, and didn't return home for several days? Do you find yourself looking at your teen with anger but with thoughts like "I know I should forgive because you're doing better. But how *could* you do that to us?"

A recovering adult once mentioned that he accepts the fact that his friends and family still hold some grudges about his chemically dependent behavior. After apologizing and making amends, he knows that all he can do now is to act responsibly and sensitively toward those he wronged. It's very human to hold grudges. So how do you move on and refuse to let anger ruin the good life your family is now working so hard to keep?

Your best course of action is to hold a family meeting to air lingering resentments openly. If you're feeling anxious, fear a bad outcome, or feel you need support to keep the conversation at the meeting safe and appropriate, invite a therapist to be present. At your meeting, deal with four orders of business: (1) encourage everyone to express and listen to all past resentments; (2) help everyone learn to forgive—but not forget—the wrongs of others; (3) have everyone express at least one thing he or she appreciates about every other family member; and (4) involve the whole family in doing something fun together. By means of a family meeting, everyone in the family can put lingering resentments behind, respect what has happened, but see that the future holds greater promise and hope.

Support Groups. As you begin to feel more balanced, you may find less need to rely on others to keep you going and give you hope. However, don't forget that a support group helped you get where you are today. You and your friends in your support group will feel stronger and more optimistic when you let those who stuck by you know how well you're doing. Remember, too, that there are probably some new members in your support group who are feeling as tired, empty, scared, and depressed as you once did. They need to know how you survived, healed, and strengthened yourself. You can be a source of courage and hope for them. For the same reasons, continue to support your teenager's ongoing involvement in his or her support system (sponsor, Alcoholics Anonymous, Narcotics Anonymous, or other groups). If an argument breaks out at home over curfew, friends, grades, or other limits, it's good to know that your child can immediately talk to others who can provide sound feedback and support.

Other Personal Problems. As your teen gets well, you have more time for yourself and your own personal issues may begin to surface. When they do, it's not unusual for you to start feeling worse. To improve your own and your family's health you have to face your own painful emotions, memories of hurts, missed opportunities, and, perhaps, chemical dependence. If issues like these crop up and make it too difficult for you to carry out your daily schedule, seek professional help. You deserve it. At the very least, you deserve someone just to sit and listen to what you've gone through.

ANSWERS TO QUESTIONS PARENTS ASK

The following questions are typical of ones that parents frequently ask during the Consistency and Balance Stage.

Why should my teen have other emotional problems now that he or she isn't using alcohol and other drugs? Other kids of that age don't have these troubles.

This question points up how unfair the disease of chemical dependence can be. Staying sober and straight requires real courage. Sometimes, however, it's not enough to bring about recovery. Some adolescents are very chaotic and out of control when they're using alcohol or other drugs. During recovery, they become organized and healthy. Many anti-social and destructive behaviors disappear. But other teens (about 20 to 40 percent of chemically dependent adolescents) may have used alcohol or other drugs to control or repress devastating thoughts, feelings, and behaviors. When these teens stop using alcohol or other drugs, these old problems may resurface. Then these teens become more troubled, anti-social, and destructive and require ongoing help to prevent regressing into active chemical dependence.

Now that my child is really progressing, isn't it time to get off the psychiatric medications and not have to rely on them to survive?

This is a good question but difficult to answer, because it really depends on the particular teen. Psychiatric medications could have been prescribed to keep down cravings, rage attacks, depression, anxiety, or other turbulent states during recovery's Stability and Structure Stage. Once the teen learns enough social skills and builds enough confidence to apply those skills, you can discuss with the psychiatrist whether medications can stop. Some psychiatric conditions, however, may require several years of medication in order to prevent a relapse.

Some recovering teens complain that they continue to need medication because they feel sad, unhappy, or depressed. They may really be saying, "I know I'm doing well, but maybe by hanging onto this medication I'll be guaranteed that I'll never go backward again."

Such a teen needs reassurance regarding two things. First, it takes time and experience to build confidence in handling life's challenges. Medicine can help keep certain feelings, thoughts, and actions from getting out of control, but the rest is up to the teen. Second, it's normal to feel angry, sad, depressed, fearful, and unhappy at times because the disease of chemical dependence can make a recovering person feel that there's something wrong with having these feelings. The teen needs to realize that whether medication remains necessary, he or she will still have to deal with life's challenges and uncomfortable feelings like any other person.

What should I do if my child fights the recovery plan—for example, by stopping therapy, cutting back on self-help group meetings, or breaking family rules? Will this defiance throw us back into the same place or trouble we were in before we got help?

Answers to this question can vary, depending on the teenager and the family. Here are four possibilities:

1. Your child could be suffering a relapse. Check with others in your teen's "safety net" to see whether they have the same fears as you. If so, form an action plan with those people and get ready to set specific limits for your teen. These limits should relate directly to their behavior. So, for example, if your teen ignores your evening curfew, you can limit his or her free time with friends. But remember: Don't panic. Being

consistent and balanced requires steady thinking, feeling, and problem solving.

2. If your teen often acts "sneaky" to get his or her way, you may be asking for trouble if you're not keeping the recovery plan up to date. Hold a family meeting to revise the plan, and get advice from your therapist and support groups.

3. Perhaps your teen is simply testing your authority again. Remember, *all* teens normally test parental limits to see whether you're serious about them and whether they can get away with being a bit sneaky. Get back to basics. Discuss again with your teen the reasons for the rules in the recovery plan. Your child may simply be trying to choose ways to be independent but has simply chosen the wrong ways—defying the recovery plan—to try his or her wings.

4. Finally, consider the possibility that your teen really is ready to become independent but that you might be holding him or her back. Sure, defying the recovery plan is unacceptable behavior. Perhaps your child is defiant because you're unwilling to let go even when he or she is being trustworthy. As we've already seen, it's normal for you to feel a bit anxious about how your life will change when your child becomes independent. So don't worry so much about a child who's doing well. Instead, focus more attention on your own health and needs for fulfillment.

CHAPTER 4

STAGE FOUR: ATTACHMENT

In stage four of recovery, attachment, the accomplishments of the first three stages start to pay off. There's significantly less uproar and much more cooperation and understanding within the family. Honest discussion about school, careers, friendships, religion, and politics becomes the normal way of life. Now everyone's major goal becomes how to attach to people in a fulfilling and respectful way. It's far more desirable and life-giving to attach to people than to alcohol and other drugs.

THE PROBLEMS YOUR TEENAGER FACES
This isn't to say that your teen won't have to deal with some problems during this recovery stage. Generally, teens face two major problems in stage four: handling needs for independence, and dealing with the possibility of a relapse.

Even after achieving and maintaining consistency and balance, some teens may decide to back out of individual, group, or family therapy. If you see this happening with your teen, you may feel frustrated and wonder why this would happen to a young person who's just beginning to cope maturely with life's problems and difficulties.

Look at such "backing out" behavior from a new perspective. Namely, your teen may in fact be acting maturely by facing up to the challenges of independence. In other words, like all teens, recovering teens need to test themselves out in the real world without the pressure of adults, even caring adults who are trying to help. Your teen may reckon that facing the challenge of independence is more important than solving other long-term problems he or she may still have: for example, abuse, neglect, depression, or self-defeating behavior.

If you know that your recovering teen generally acts with consistency and balance, don't panic. Your teen's therapist will let go for the time being, but keep the door open for future therapy and keep in touch with your teen. A recovering older adolescent needs to say, "I need to get out on my own, but I'll come back when I really need help." Allow your teen to say and do this.

In spite of a youngster's many achievements in recovery thus far, a relapse is still possible. Why? First of all, everyone has a breaking point, those trying times when all a person wants is for everyone to leave him or her alone. If stress become overwhelming, the weakest part of the person will break down. For a chemically dependent person, this can mean a return to using alcohol or other drugs. In the fourth stage of recovery, such a "breakdown" with a return to chemical use is less likely to happen, but it's not impossible.

The second reason why a relapse is possible, even at this recovery stage, is because a chemically dependent person never needs a reason to use alcohol or other drugs again. This is the baffling mystery of the disease of chemical dependence. No matter how much progress a teen makes in recovery, it will not stop them from wanting to use alcohol or other drugs. That desire to use will always be with them.

Behaviors to Expect from Your Teenager

For the most part, the behaviors you can expect from your teenager during stage four are wonderful ones. You'll see your adolescent acting more and more like a mature young adult—the sort of person you've always hoped he or she would become. He or she is more confident, has better problem-solving skills, and can cope with difficult feelings and challenges. You'll notice that your child sees you in a new light as well, as someone who has wisdom to share, wisdom based on real-life experience. Your child will no longer accuse you of letting him or her down. Instead, your son or daughter will accept your strengths and your weaknesses, recognizing that both are part of what it means to be an adult.

THE PROBLEMS PARENTS FACE

For the most part, the problems you will face during this fourth stage of recovery will be quite manageable. To begin, you'll have to make some adjustments as your teenager moves from being "your little child" to "your young adult." Once your teen has made this move, he or she will no longer see you as a boat to carry him or her *through* life's storm, but as a brief refuge *from* the storm—someone he or she can come to for a rest, get a good meal, or find help with laundry should money run out before the next paycheck. Occasionally, you may even find your teen turning to you for advice on how to deal with work or school pressures, relationships, or financial difficulties.

In addition, you will have time to concentrate on your own development: on your marriage, finances, careers, spiritual lives, and physical health. At this stage, some parents may need to seek counseling regarding these issues, but all the while retaining strong faith that, with devotion to the job ahead, life can and will improve.

ATTACHMENT TASKS FOR THE TEEN

There are six tasks the recovering teen must accomplish during this stage of recovery. They resemble the steps of Alcoholics Anonymous (AA), with emphasis on the last seven. (See page 125, for a complete listing of the Twelve Steps.) Put in the teenager's own words, these tasks are as follows:

1. "I know what my relapse warning signs[6] are. I know what to do and when to get help." (AA Steps 1, 2, and 3)

2. "I am using the steps of Alcoholics Anonymous and Narcotics Anonymous every day." Briefly, these steps focus on:

- preparing and then humbly asking for help in removing one's personality defects (AA Steps 6 and 7)
- preparing and then making amends to those persons one has wronged (AA Steps 8 and 9)
- continuing to evaluate one's life and to admit wrongdoing immediately (AA Step 10)
- continuing to understand one's need for a higher power (AA Step 11)
- having the willingness to devote time to help others who are suffering from chemical dependence (AA Step 12)

3. "I don't run away from my emotional problems, my learning disabilities, or my difficulties with relating to others. I've got to face them." (AA Steps 1 to 5)

4. "I really want to know why I do what I do and what I can do to change myself. Getting help and treatment doesn't make me weak. It makes me strong." (AA Step 10)

5. "I want to help others who have problems with alcohol and other drugs. I have the energy and the time to do so. When I help others, I help myself, because I remember the hard work I've done." (AA Step 12)

---

[6] These warning signs are discussed thoroughly in Chapter 5.

6. "I'm really getting to know who I am and what I want out of life. Now I can begin to make plans for leaving home and for supporting myself." (AA Steps 1 to 12)

Alcohol and other drugs had ruined your teen's chances for getting close to others in any meaningful way. Attachment to others is something we all need and all need to do. It's part of who we are to need to be attached, connected to others and to the world around us. With such connection and attachment no one is boxed in. On the contrary, everyone has room to express feelings, get needs met, and state opinions without fear of humiliation. That's why these attachment tasks are crucial ones for your teen to accomplish.

Thankfully, by means of the Twelve Steps, Alcoholics Anonymous and Narcotics Anonymous teach an ordered approach for staying sober and straight and for attaching to others that is both fulfilling and healthy. The Twelve Steps help your teen not only to become aware of problems, but to change and become a healthier person, all at the same time.

RECOVERY FACTORS FOR PARENTS TO REMEMBER

As you watch your teenager progressing, accomplishing the tasks of this stage, and making new and stronger attachments, there are seven important principles of recovery that you, as parents, should keep in mind.

1. *Recovery is a delicate balancing act.* When it comes to recovery, the family lives in fragile balance. On the one side is the chaos and destructiveness of chemical dependence. On the other is the slow and difficult practice of living in a healthy manner. Sharon Wegscheider-Cruse, who pioneered family recovery at the Johnson Institute, describes alcohol or other drugs as another member of the family that intrudes and threatens the family, and that must be thrown out lest the family lose its balance altogether.

2. *No family member stands alone.* One of the most important recent insights into chemical dependence is that it is indeed a *family* disease. Some experts call this family disease *co-dependence* because those closest to the chemical dependent commonly suffer wide-ranging psychological damage and often become as emotionally distressed as the chemically dependent person. In fact, it's nearly impossible for those around a practicing chemical dependent not to be drawn into the sickness. Such persons are apt to become anxious and fearful and to develop feelings of low self-worth, fear, anger, resentment, and shame. In other words, they're likely to develop their own emotional illness in connection with another's chemical dependence. Often their emotional pain shows in physical symptoms, including headaches, stomachaches, and ulcers. As a result, they too need help in dealing with the problem.

3. *Healthy families learn how to be stable and secure.* Recovering families must learn how to talk in ways that build trust; how to solve problems in ways that give hope; how to respect one another and to encourage personal growth.

4. *Recovery takes work.* By now you know the truth of this statement. Chemical dependence can seem to be an "easy" way to live in the world, but it's a very dangerous one. For a chemically dependent person, genuine ease comes only from completing the recovery tasks of each stage and from working hard to manage one's feelings, thoughts, behavior, and relationships. To take healthy risks, make the right choices, and retain hope for the future take courage and wisdom. And courage and wisdom take hard work.

5. *You must keep support alive.* Recovery is impossible without support. You need to continue to support your teen, and get support for yourself from other families who share your problems. To accept and extend support makes the human struggle successful and worthwhile.

6. *Teenagers have never been easy to understand.* It's difficult to know what is healthy, normal behavior for adolescents and what is not. Often your adolescent won't know either. Have patience. Familiarize

yourselves with the recovery tasks of your teen, and help where you can. This may involve getting your child to group meetings on time and being available—physically and emotionally—to your teen.

7. *Treatment programs need your help.* Treatment is a two-way street. A family can't get help unless it admits there is a problem. Each family member needs to understand and be willing to change any behavior patterns that keep problems going. Each family member also needs to learn how to improve family life and to express in an appropriate manner any unmet needs. Professional helpers need to hear and know that you believe in the possibility of change for the better. At the same time, you need to recognize what professional helpers can realistically do for you and your child. To help treatment be more effective and to help you get what you need from it, keep in mind the following questions to ask therapists as treatment progresses:

- What are my child's problems?
- What are my family's problems that keep my child's problems going?
- What is your treatment plan for my adolescent and my family?
- From what program should we seek help now? What program in the future?
- What are the goals of this program and the goals of the next program, once we're finished here?
- What tasks should we complete in this program?
- What tasks should be completed in the next program?

If you keep these seven factors in mind, not only your teen, but every member of your family will grow, change, and become a healthier individual.

CHAPTER 5

HOW YOU CAN HELP IF YOUR TEEN RELAPSES

Chemical dependence is a disease that can be arrested but that can never be fully cured. That's why we stress that recovery is continuous and ongoing—a process, not an event. Therefore, when you hear chemical dependence professionals talking about "relapse prevention," they're talking about managing the problems that can occur during the process of recovery from chemical dependence.

WHAT IS RELAPSE?

The typical dictionary defines relapse as a steady decline or falling back into a former worse state. In terms of chemical dependence, then, a relapse is not something that happens in a day or an instant. Thus, a recovering teen who on one occasion drinks one beer may have "slipped" but has not necessarily suffered a full-blown relapse.

However, a recovering teen can relapse without ever using alcohol or drugs again. Relapse may be predicated on chemical use, but chemical use is not necessarily a condition for relapse to take place. Remember that any deteriorating behavior can signal the beginning of relapse. The relapse process takes place in three stages and has definite warning signs that can be recognized and monitored.

Stage One: Relapse Stress Reaction

Generally, relapse begins when a teen begins to feel very stressed out and is unable to deal with those anxious feelings. The teen finds himself or herself overwhelmed with the normal problems and challenges of life, viewing them as too much to bear, and feeling as if their world were falling apart. In professional circles, this stress reaction is now being called either the "prolonged abstinence syndrome" or "post-acute withdrawal."

What sort of stress can trigger this reaction? To answer, let's first of all agree on what "stress" means. Stress is anything—a person, place, thing, time, event, and so on—that a person perceives will require or bring about *change*. Stress is change, and change is often difficult to deal with. When such stress occurs, the normal operations of a recovering teen's brain can short out or fail. The young person may be experiencing a number of jumbled feelings that no one can understand, least of all the teen. How can you help? Ask your teen what he or she is feeling, but don't be surprised if the answer you get is unclear. To get a handle on what your child is really feeling, you need to learn how to interpret his or her responses.

Below are some typical responses or statements recovering teens experiencing a stress reaction may make. After each statement is a list of "interpretations" to help you understand what sort of emotions your child may be experiencing.

"I can't think straight."
- My mind keeps racing.
- I can't get certain thoughts out of my head (for example, thoughts of suicide, failing, wanting to use alcohol or other drugs again).
- I can't seem to solve problems.
- I can't understand why I act the way I do.
- I can't understand what I read or what I'm told.
- On any given day, I don't know what to do first for myself.
- I don't even understand what other people say to each other.

"I can't pin down how I feel."
- Sometimes I overreact to the smallest irritations.
- Sometimes I show no feelings, even though I should.
- Sometimes I know that I feel something, but I don't know what it is.
- Sometimes I think I should feel one way, but I feel another.

"I can't remember things and concentrate."
- My mind seems to wander a lot.
- I'm always daydreaming.
- I can't remember something that just happened—or that happened a long time ago.
- I can't remember anything new I learn in school or at work.

"When I'm really stressed out, my thinking, feeling, remembering, and concentrating get worse. When the stress is gone, I feel okay."
- I'm in trouble.
- Help!

Stage Two: Relapse Warning Signs

In the second stage of the relapse process, the teenager begins to show a number of trouble signs. If your teen begins to exhibit any of the signs listed below, or if you notice more than one of these signs in combination, your child may be headed toward a relapse.

- Emotional signs
- Thinking signs
- Behavioral signs

Emotional Signs. The most common distressful emotions are anger, sadness, fear, rage, self-hate, and emptiness. Look for signs of these emotions in your teenager's facial expressions and body posture (such as tightness or slouching). These emotions seem quite overwhelming to an early recovering teen. He or she may try to mask them behind self-pity and loneliness or by acting silly or throwing a temper tantrum. Over time, repressed feelings can lead to depression and emotional tension or anxiety.

Thinking Signs. A teenager who is about to relapse will complain of mental confusion. You may notice that he or she can't solve everyday problems, won't make necessary plans for the future, comes up with simplistic answers that don't work, tries to convince you that the problem is unimportant, or "awfulizes" the problem, that is, makes it look worse than it actually is.

During conversations, your teen will have trouble contributing personal thoughts or won't be able to follow what others are saying. Your child may also appear to be daydreaming too much, which is really a form of wanting rewards without working for them. Thoughts of suicide, homicide, or other forms of violence often worsen this mental confusion.

Behavioral Signs. Four behaviors generally indicate the possibility or relapse: (1) avoidance, (2) hostility, (3) impulsiveness, and (4) minor physical illness.

Avoidance has many faces. It can reveal itself when your child tries to change the subject of emotionally upsetting conversations. Likewise, in relationships, your youngster may avoid dealing with stress by acting "too good." Your teen will give good advice to family and friends but won't reveal any personal thoughts or feelings. Being "too good" has gone too far when your child becomes overly obedient or seeks the approval of others too much.

Another face of avoidance is social withdrawal or awkwardness, which shows up especially in the teen who is being teased or put down a lot. Fearing the laughter or derision of peers, the recovering adolescent avoids standing up for himself or herself.

Avoidance is acted out in treatment. You may hear your child evade the need for help by saying, "I'll never drink again" or "I won't use like before." Avoidance is also acted out when a youngster assists others more than himself or herself, is absent or tardy, stalls in finding a sponsor or in completing recovery tasks, spends time with drug-using friends, wants to cut down time in treatment (especially during early recovery), never shares painful feelings during therapy, or agrees to follow advice but never follows through.

Hostility is revealed by a teen's intense arguing, swearing, sarcasm, playing pranks, resentments, physical threats, and violent actions. In treatment a hostile teenager may be *actively* defiant: "Make me!" "I won't!" "Yes, but...you don't understand...nobody does." A hostile teen may also be *passively* defiant: "I won't make trouble. Just leave me alone," or look angry but refuse to speak.

Impulsiveness means acting too quickly without considering possible consequences. An impulsive teenager won't have a daily schedule. He or she will make promises but forget to fulfill them. Poor grades in school, tardiness, absences, and suspensions are common. The teen changes or abandons friends. In treatment, the youngster acts inconsistently. The young person does poorly even though he or she has the potential to do well or falls apart right after agreeing to a family contract that should work.

The final behavioral sign indicating a possible relapse is minor physical illness. Look for your child exhibiting headaches, muscle pains, stomachaches, back aches, chronic coughs, constipation, persistent colds. These problems appear when your youngster is not successfully managing stress.

Stage Three: Actual Relapse

As we said earlier, relapse is not something that happens in a day or an instant, but is a process. The relapse process, therefore, can culminate in a number of ways. When preceded by the stress reactions and warning signs outlined above, any of the six major problems listed below can signal relapse.

- *Experimenting with Alcohol or Other Drug Use*
- *Psychological Disorders*: depression, anxiety attacks, phobias, psychosis, eating disorders, attention deficits, suicidal or homicidal behavior, explosive disorders
- *Constant Fatigue*
- *Major Medical Illness*
- *Poor Judgment and Carelessness Leading to Accidents*
- *Worsening of All the Above Problems*

FACTS ABOUT RELAPSE

Over the past ten years, assessment and treatment of adolescent chemical dependence have progressed a long way. Still, professionals don't know enough about how to help teenagers achieve permanent sobriety. The Ramsey Clinic in St. Paul, Minnesota, examined adolescent relapse and recovery through its CATOR (Chemical Assessment Treatment Outcome Registry) study of mostly shorter-term treatment centers. CATOR focused on teenagers one year after treatment to determine recovery rates, and, therefore, relapse rates as well. The CATOR findings, which are summarized below, may serve as a guide to determining treatment effectiveness with an eye to raising recovery rates and preventing relapse. However, you should not read these findings as strict rules about how treatment should happen. Rather, simply see them as offering some insights into relapse that can help you as you help your teen recover.

Teenagers relapse more often than adults. After a year, a smaller percentage of adolescents than adults remains free of alcohol or other drugs. It appears that a younger age and the use of more types of drugs increase the chance of relapse. Maturity does make a difference in recovering.

Staying free of drugs is difficult—most teens relapse. Only 44 percent of teens were abstinent after one year, while 33 percent had multiple relapses and 23 percent had a brief relapse. You should be prepared for your child to relapse.

Girls and boys have different recovery rates. Girls remain abstinent more than boys (50 percent versus 40 percent). Boys report multiple relapses more than girls (39 percent versus 26 percent).

Associating with non-using friends helps recovery. Affiliating with friends who avoid alcohol and other drugs improves a teenager's chances of staying free of chemicals by a margin of 41 percent.

Completing treatment prevents relapse. Teens who completed a short-term program were more likely to remain abstinent after a year than teens who left the program early. Still, only 50 percent of those who did complete treatment remained abstinent, versus 30 percent of those who failed to complete it. This finding points out that it's important to complete a treatment program, but relapse can still occur. However, three out of four teens who completed a program *and then completed an aftercare program* as well remained free of chemicals after one year.

Attending self-help groups helps prevent relapse. Youngsters who stayed involved in Alcoholics Anonymous or other self-help groups throughout the year (65 percent of them) were more likely to stay alcohol- and other drug-free. When attendance dropped below two meetings per month, relapse became more probable.

Most recovering teenagers also suffer from other psychiatric problems requiring treatment. Eight out of ten recovering youngsters had two or more serious problems besides chemical dependence. The CATOR study discovered that the most common problems were with school, parents, parental chemical dependence, physical abuse, depression, and the law. Teens also had problems with sexual abuse, learning disabilities, suicidal tendencies, poor self-image, and problem-sharing. Girls were more likely to relapse if, in the previous year, they had attempted suicide, suffered from depression, or been physically abused. Relapses were also more likely in cases where legal problems were present.

Parents involved in support groups can help prevent relapse. If a parent became involved in a self-help group, the teen was likely to remain abstinent. A father's participation in such groups seemed to improve a teen's chances of avoiding relapse more than did a mother's.

WHAT PARENTS CAN DO TO HELP PREVENT RELAPSE

At first glance, the findings of the CATOR study outlined above may seem a bit depressing. You may be thinking, "Why work so hard, if relapse is all but inevitable?" Actually, you know the answer to that question: You love your child; you want to give him or her the very best chance at recovery; and you want your family to return to happiness and health.

Many people are helping you to work to that end. The CATOR study, too, can help. It points to a number of important roles that parents can play in helping their child avoid relapse.

1. Continue to rely on your supports and "safety net." You're not alone. Take part in self-help groups. And do your best to keep your teen and your family in treatment no matter what. It's your best insurance policy against relapse.

2. Learn more about the warning signs of relapse. Remember when your teen was a baby or toddler how much attention you paid to his or her habits (eating, sleeping, toilet) and development (crawling, walking, talking)? Become as interested in your recovering teen's habits and development as you were when he or she was an infant. Children act in healthier ways when they feel that their parents are interested in them and understand them.

3. See to it that your teen's treatment program teaches, or knows where your teen can learn, new social skills, relaxation skills, stress management, and relapse prevention.

4. Let your child know if you think a problem is developing that may lead him or her to relapse.

5. Gather as much information as you can about your child's thoughts, feelings, behavior, and relationships.

6. When you set consequences, make them practical and based on the belief that setting limits with consequences are normal things that people do.

7. Continue to demonstrate your care and concern about your child's struggle. At the same time, however, learn to detach *yourself* from your teen's relapse. In other words, don't let your emotions rise and fall with your youngster's struggle. If the situation is to get better, someone has to evidence some control. Your teen—even if he or she does, in fact, relapse—needs to see that you can stay cool and supportive. Again, remember your support network. Turn to them for your own emotional support.

CHAPTER 6

TREATMENT PROGRAMS

In the previous chapter you saw that completing treatment helps to prevent relapse. Earlier, in Chapter 2, you discovered that professional help or a treatment program is crucial to creating a good recovery plan for your teenager. Treatment programs may be short-term, intermediate, or long-term. Below, you'll find each type of program described and discussed. A good program will have a specialized approach to treating chemical dependence and will work on all the recovery tasks described elsewhere in this book.

SHORT-TERM PROGRAMS

Short-term programs have three goals: (1) to identify and understand problems; (2) to stabilize the teenager, allowing him or her to benefit from help with fewer restrictions; and (3) to foster the creation of a recovery plan before leaving the program.

Crisis or Runaway Shelters

These shelters are found in many communities. Teens often find such settings helpful to cool off when they're having trouble living at home. Having their teen stay temporarily in safe shelter also gives parents time to find a more intensive or structured program if this is necessary.

The Outpatient Assessment Program

Most chemical dependence professionals provide outpatient assessment services at their offices. Count on using this service when you are in the Crisis Control Stage, that is, when you are simply trying to find out if your teen has a problem serious enough to warrant a more intensive program. Specialists, such as psychiatrists or psychologists, may be called in to help determine the question of "dual diagnosis" (see page 7).

The Inpatient Assessment and Brief Treatment Program

This program can be found in general and psychiatric hospitals and in some free-standing chemical dependence treatment facilities. It should address the Stability and Structure Stage of recovery and its tasks. The length of a teen's stay in such a program varies from one week to six weeks. Generally, you should not expect all the goals of stage two to be realized in such a short period of time.

INTERMEDIATE PROGRAMS

When teens successfully complete a short-term program but are not yet ready to function at home with their families, a therapeutic group home can be just the right place to complete the tasks of the Consistency and Balance Stage (stage three) of recovery. The therapeutic group home encourages sobriety, teaches social skills for dealing with peer pressure, and prepares teens for living with the family again. A typical length of stay is three to six months. These homes are also called "halfway" or "quarterway" houses.

LONG-TERM PROGRAMS

The Residential Treatment Program

There are at least three types of residential treatment programs:

- psychiatric hospital
- "dual diagnosis" residential
- chemical dependence residential

The psychiatric hospital program treats "dual diagnosis" adolescents with very severe psychiatric and chemical dependence problems. The "dual diagnosis" residential program serves teenagers who can calm themselves and control their behavior, and who need fewer limits and rules. The chemical dependence residential program helps teens who do not have other severe emotional problems.

Teens in all three settings have usually been through other treatment programs, consistently fail in spite of their potential for success, and continue to relapse. These teens tend to become involved in destructive relationships and get into trouble repeatedly, never seeming to learn from their mistakes. After living with so much chaos and conflict, the families of these teens need more confidence and experience to welcome their teenager back home and into the family. Usually, the residential treatment program focuses on the tasks of the Stability and Structure and the Consistency and Balance stages of recovery.

The Outpatient Treatment Program

Some adolescents can go directly from crisis or short-term programs into an intensive outpatient program, while living at home. There are several reasons for placing a teen in an outpatient program. First, a highly motivated teenager is likely to comply with the rules of home, avoid their chemical-using friends, and can be easily tested in the outpatient setting. Second, although an adolescent may need a residential treatment setting, some families can afford only an outpatient program. Third, some families are not ready for a residential program; they still may not believe that their youngster's problems are that severe and may insist on trying outpatient first.

Generally in outpatient programs teens work three or four evenings and one weekend day a week to accomplish the tasks of the second and third stages of recovery. The drawback to such programs is that professional staff and parents usually work overtime to handle crises that could be either prevented or handled more efficiently by trained staff in a residential program.

The Day Treatment Program

The "dual diagnosis" teenager, who can live at home but who needs more support and therapy, can use this program. Some day treatment programs require the teenager to live with another family (not his or her own), until the teen completes certain Stability and Structure tasks. The teenager attends school at or away from the treatment facility. About one-quarter to one-half of teens in a day treatment program require psychiatric medications for stability.

Day treatment program staff include psychiatrists, psychologists, social workers, and chemical dependence counselors. Graduation from the program takes place after the teen successfully completes the tasks of the Consistency and Balance Stage of recovery.

The Therapeutic School Program

Similar to a day treatment program, a therapeutic school treats the "dual diagnosis" adolescent. Social workers, counselors, and teachers provide most of the ongoing support. Independent outpatient therapists may also consult with the program and provide teens any required psychotherapy. School is conducted at the facility. Usually, adolescents in such a program are more organized and need less support than those in day treatment. Therapeutic school programs best help teens who have reached the third recovery stage, Consistency and Balance.

The Self-help Program

Alcoholics Anonymous, Narcotics Anonymous, Cocaine Anonymous, and other similar self-help groups are crucial to teens in every stage of recovery. On occasion, a teen may get sober by participating only in A.A. Usually, a sponsor is supporting the teenager. Generally, self-help programs become the sole support for a youngster only when he or she has reached the last stage of recovery, the Attachment Stage.

No matter which treatment program you and your teen take part in, it is extremely important for you to have a detailed recovery plan, to follow it well, and to review it often. When a teen is out of a treatment program, living at home again, and a crisis happens, parents need follow only three simple rules: (1)   Don't panic! (2)   Don't panic!! (3)   Don't panic!!! When you're scared or frustrated by what appears to be a serious problem, remember that others can help you solve the problem. So ask for help.

CHAPTER 7

HOW PARENTS CAN HELP THEMSELVES

By now you've recognized that chemical dependence is a family disease, that everyone in the family is affected by it. The overall goal of this book is to help you help your chemically dependent teen recover, but your recovery is no less important than your teen's. Thus, as you read this chapter, you'll see that some of the material discussed herein has necessarily been discussed earlier in the book.

PERSONAL RECOVERY

One of the most effective ways for families to recover from chemical dependence is offered by the two self-help groups Al-Anon and Families Anonymous. Each offers a twelve-step prescription for recovery that enables participants to find some serenity and stability in their own lives. Six general principles underlie the steps:

1. Recognizing powerlessness and unmanageability
2. Finding support

3. Admitting shortcomings
4. Healing
5. Developing a relationship with a "higher power"
6. Helping others

We'll examine each of these principles to discover how following them can help lead you to personal recovery.

Recognize That You're Powerless over Your Teen's Chemical Dependence and That Your Life Has Become Unmanageable (Al-Anon Step 1)

Your teen's chemical dependence is not your fault. You cannot stop it. You cannot change his or her behavior. Even professional therapists cannot "fix" your child and return your life to normal. As good and caring parents, you've taken on the responsibility of your teen's disease and done everything you possibly can to help your troubled teenager grow and change. But know this: Using alcohol and other drugs won't let him or her change. They prevent your teen's mind and body from functioning and developing normally. You cannot stop your teen from using alcohol and other drugs. You are *powerless.*

Recognizing that you are powerless may at first seem depressing. Many parents feel that they've failed their child and their family. They think, "Well, what's the use of even trying to be a parent? Are we supposed to let our kid go down the tubes? If our teen isn't in control of his or her life, we have to be, right?" Wrong.

Think a moment of what your life with a chemically dependent teen has been like: shouting, insulting, punishing, arguing. Has that kind of *control* helped? None of these controlling behaviors has ever stopped a teenager from getting high, stoned, or drunk. Should you abandon your role as parents? Absolutely not. As parents you need to continue good parenting: setting limits and allowing your teen to suffer the consequences of alcohol or other drug use. What you *do* need to abandon, however, is any notion that you can control your teen's behavior. Recognizing that you're powerless means learning to "detach" your feelings and thoughts from your teen's behavior. Detachment does not mean abandoning your teen. On the contrary, one way of detaching is to realize that your child needs help right away, but that he or she can't get it if your own disturbed thoughts, feelings, or actions are in the way. As paradoxical as it may sound, admitting that you're powerless is empowering. It empowers you, your teen, and your family to get the help you all so urgently need.

Confronted with the disappointments and failures of dealing with a chemically dependent teen, normal parents turn their attention and energies away from all else and focus them on their troubled child. Now is the time for some refocusing. Remember, everyone in your family is affected by your teen's disease. Everyone in your family will need attention to recover from the disease. (*Note:* The topic of family recovery is discussed later in this chapter.)

Imagine for a moment that your teen's disease isn't chemical dependence, but that he or she had strep throat. Just as you would have other members of your family examined to see whether they were getting strep throat, so should you check to see whether the disease of chemical dependence is affecting other family members. Stresses from job, school, work, finances, and so on can render the whole family more vulnerable to emotional and physical illnesses, including psychological problems and chemical dependence itself. This is what we mean by *unmanageability.* No one can manage a life plagued by chemical dependence. You can, however, help yourselves and family members recognize unmanageability, realize that healing is required, and seek help and support to begin coping effectively.

Find a Support Group: Recognize and Accept Something Greater than Yourself That Can Guide You in Troubled or Peaceful Times (Al-Anon Steps 2 & 3)

In a support group, you and your family can find your own "higher power" to help you cope with the many difficulties of chemical dependence. So supported, many parents are able to renew spiritual beliefs and practices. Finding a connection with a higher power can give you faith that life will improve and that you will feel at home again in the world.

Admit How You Kept Your Family and Yourselves from Healing (Al-Anon Step 4)

Remember that your teen's chemical dependence is not your fault. This step toward personal recovery, then, is not about admitting responsibility for your teen's alcohol or other drug use. It is not about accepting blame for your child's chemical dependence. It is, however, a difficult step for parents to take, because it means taking responsibility for personal and family problems and admitting that your way of dealing with your behavior and feelings could be improved.

Most parents in the first two stages of recovery (Crisis Control and Stability and Structure) struggle mightily to manage their feelings. They feel enraged, humiliated, or fearful when anyone explores or questions their behavior, feelings, thinking, and relationships. Sometimes, parents who are called upon to spend so much time behaving like adults still have a hurt child trapped inside. If that child grew up being depressed, traumatized, abused, or in a chaotic family, life as an adult can be very unstable.

Heal Yourself and Your Family with Humility, Honesty, and Courage (Al-Anon Steps 6-10)

The healing we're speaking about here is really the same as accomplishing the tasks of the third stage of recovery, finding consistency and balance in your life. To effect such healing, you need to mend the painful and overpowering feelings and to change the destructive behaviors that rule your family. To do this, you need to give yourselves time: time to humbly rethink how past feelings, actions, and behaviors have not honestly solved problems but have resulted in more family chaos; time to muster the courage to make amends to those you have hurt. Given time, humility, honesty, and courage, you'll gradually find new fulfillment in your family, relationships, and work. You'll find healing.

Continue to Enrich Your Relationship to a Higher Power (Al-Anon Step 11)

Once you begin to heal old wounds, mend everyday life, and make amends for painful past behavior, you can begin to live contentedly. You'll see that your connections to others, your relationships, and your spiritual life will continue to grow. You're becoming healthily *attached* to the world, recognizing that you are part of it, and that you care about—and can do something about—keeping it alive and well.

Come to the Aid of Other Teens and Families Who Are Suffering (Al-Anon Step 12)

Self-help groups like Al-Anon, upon whose Twelve Steps all these principles of coming to personal recovery are based, recognize that helping others is impossible without first helping oneself. You can't give what you haven't got. Your personal and family's healing and health must come first. With experience and time, however, you'll find the energy, commitment, and wherewithal to reach out to others who need the help you once desired. Such caring outreach doesn't signal the end of personal recovery, only crowns it. (At the end of this book you'll find a resource list of books on chemical dependence and recovery.)

Some families have difficulty accepting the culture of self-help groups like Al-Anon and Families Anonymous. They may have difficulty talking in front of people, find that these groups feel too "religious" for their personal tastes, or simply be unable to pin down what makes them feel uncomfortable with self-help groups.

If you find that you share similar feelings, recognize that there is no single "right" way to recovery and to living a fulfilling life in this world. However, many people do find true contentment by following the principles outlined above (recognizing powerlessness and unmanageability; finding support; admitting shortcomings; healing; enriching relationship to a "higher power"; and reaching out to help others). These principles or guidelines lead to healing, but they can be found outside of self-help groups: through religious organizations, friends, counselors, community activities, personal study, meditation, and so on. If you have difficulty with a particular self-help group, look for another one, one that speaks more clearly to your heart. If you have difficulty with the whole notion of self-help groups, don't reject the principles so well embodied in their twelve steps. They can lead you to personal recovery.

FAMILY RECOVERY

Just as an individual possesses a personality with strengths and weaknesses, so does a family. Many qualities contribute to a family's personality: family rules, successes and failures; a family's philosophy of child-rearing; the type or style of marriage the parents have; the family's problem-solving style; the sexes and ages of family members. The family's personality changes as family members—children and adults—become more independent. As each family member grows into a fuller person, the family should benefit and feel safer.

A teenager who is out of control due to chemical dependence weakens a family, alters its personality. As we've seen earlier, no one in a family escapes the hurt of chemical dependence.

When it comes to family recovery, four requirements are necessary:
1. Being willing to receive treatment
2. Creating healthy family roles
3. Creating a healthy family structure
4. Maintaining a healthy marital relationship; or maintaining yourself as a healthy single, divorced, or remarried parent

In the sections that follow, we'll look closely at each of these requirements for family recovery.

Willingness to Receive Treatment

William Swift, a psychiatrist at the University of Wisconsin, describes four phases that families experience when seeking help. At each phase, the family asks a question that has a hidden meaning. Due to the family's fear of humiliation, hurt, disappointment, and anger, it seeks to hide behind the questions. To recover, the family must discover and accept the real meanings behind the questions it asks in each phase.

Phase 1: Denial and Despair. In this phase the family asks the helping professional, "There really isn't a problem, is there?" This question attempts to hide the family's denial and history of despair. It really means, "We are sure that we cannot be helped. Nothing can ever change, because human relationships seem dangerous and unsatisfying."

Many denying and despairing families have a history of chemical dependence or some other disorder that may go back several generations. They may also have a long history of disappointment, hurt, abuse, and poverty. Family members tend to believe that things are hopeless; life can never improve; feelings are too overwhelming; problems can never be resolved except by violence or neglect; and it's best to ignore them or deny that a problem even exists.

If your family is in this trap, how can you escape? Try to admit that compared to most other teens, your child does have a problem and might need help. Admit, too, that he or she can get the sort of help that perhaps you or others in your family never got. Seek out the aid of a professional who is able to understand and respect how trapped you feel and who can deal with your skepticism or ambivalence about really needing help.

Phase 2: Mistrust. In this phase, the family asks, "Is there really a problem?" and focuses on the child as the problem, while usually hiding other secrets. The hidden statement in this question is "If we do seek help for our child, some 'family secrets' might come out that we don't want to acknowledge or deal with." The family believes that it is more important to hide the real problems or control behavior than to understand the child's psychological state or emotional needs. The family says, in effect, "If our teen would only behave, then we wouldn't feel anxious or worried." When a therapist disagrees with the family's assessment of the situation, families tend to bristle and refuse to cooperate.

If your family is in this trap, how can you escape? Accept the fact that trusting a professional helper will not come easily. You don't have to ignore your distrust, just give yourself—and the therapist—time to deal with it. At the same time, recognize that blaming all family problems on the teen can be a way of keeping hidden certain secrets about family behavior, and this hiding of secrets can be very destructive to the family. Behaviors such as physical or sexual abuse, chemical dependence, impulsive gambling, illegal activities, neglect, and so on can never bring your family true happiness and must be brought out in the open for family members to have a chance at real recovery. Secrets like these can continue to erode family life and stability.

A family's best course is to reveal secrets like these to the therapist individually, in private, without other family members being present. This way, you can get some help with what to do about the secret problems before bringing them up with the whole family. Understand and respect that once secrets are out in the open some family members will become anxious about what might happen. That's why it's also important that all family members have the chance to admit that they have scary feelings and need time to cope with them. With a helper whom you find trustworthy, your family will be able to take more chances, open up, and find much-needed relief.

Phase 3: Guilt and Blame. Although family members may be feeling guilty for problems on the one hand, and blaming problems on other family members on the other, by the time they have reached this phase, they've accepted that their teen needs help. At this point, families ask, "What is the nature of our child's problems?" Hidden in this question is "If we cannot make our teenager the reason for all our problems, then we won't know what to do with our guilt and blame."

If you have educated, warned, and set limits for your teen about alcohol and other drugs, it makes no sense for you to feel guilty or ashamed. As we've said so often, you are not to blame for your teen's behavior. Keep in mind that most chemically dependent teens are so clever about hiding their disease that families may not know about it for a long time. In fact, when the question of the teen's possible use of alcohol or other drugs comes up, many families respond, "Our teen isn't the sort of kid who would mess around with that stuff."

But healthy and responsible parents can have a troubled teenager. As we've seen earlier, adolescence can be a very troubling time. It hits some youngsters harder than others. Thus, for some teens, using alcohol or other drugs seems an easy escape from the challenges and pain of growing up.

Guilt and blame also surface in parents who grew up with the pain of living in a chemically dependent family. Even when these parents have sworn off—or never used—alcohol and other drugs, they can be haunted by guilt over their teen's chemical dependence. If this is the case with you, stop! Don't feel guilty, and don't blame yourself.

In this phase, family members need to learn to stop blaming the teenager—or themselves—for the family's problems. At the same time, they need to take on responsibility—which is not the same as blame—for the family's health. Because your troubled teenager's problems stood out more than anyone else's in the family, he or she got help first. But everyone in your family has suffered and needs help. The family problems that you're just now discovering and admitting have probably always been there. It's just that they got worse when your teenager couldn't stop using alcohol or other drugs.

It may take you a while to realize it, but blaming only results in making another or others feel "bad." It never leads directly to real change for the better. All blame does for a family is make one member (the one doing the blaming) a winner and the rest losers.

Phase 4: Working Alliance. In the final phase of seeking help, the family has formed a working alliance with the helping person (therapist). In this phase, the family asks, "What should we (parents, teenager, sibling, and therapist) do about this problem?" Hidden within this question is another: "What kind of unforeseen hurt and pain will we have to face and survive if we want to change?" This question speaks to the sacrifice that a family must make by giving up its unhealthy roles, changing its rules and power, and facing up to any problems that may exist in the parents' marriage. Here, the therapist becomes an advisor to the family to help members find contentment and healthy living. At this phase, family members have the courage to change, but because they remain anxious and uncertain about taking risks, they still need reassurance and support.

By making themselves available and open to the help of treatment, families are able to take on the next requirement for family recovery, creating healthy roles.

Creating Healthy Family Roles

You will find unhealthy role-playing behaviors in any troubled family. But chemical dependence can cause family members to become explosive and out of control. To survive the deadly cross fire of chemical dependence, family members can develop some powerful, defensive roles to protect themselves. Sharon Wegscheider-Cruse, an expert on chemically dependent families, describes six roles[7] that family members typically assume prior to their seeking treatment:

1. The Dependent
2. The Enabler
3. The Hero
4. The Scapegoat
5. The Lost Child
6. The Mascot

Family members tend to slip into these roles because each individual is subconsciously trying to avoid some powerful feelings and because each role has a benefit or "payoff" for sticking with it. Engaging in this role-playing becomes more important for the family than honestly facing up to the chemical dependence problem.

---

[7] These roles are labels therapists use to help family members recognize unhealthy behaviors. Note that family members can slip back and forth from one role to another at different times and for different reasons.

The Dependent. This person is the chemically dependent family member, the person who is a heavy user of alcohol or other drugs. Usually it's one of the heads of the household that plays this role. But the Dependent could be your teenager. The Dependent has many reasons for not changing, and no one in the family wants to confront the person or make him or her feel any embarrassment or shame for past behavior. The payoff for the Dependent is that he or she gets to use chemicals that enable the Dependent not to have to feel any emotional pain. In time, however, the Dependent will pay the price of chemical dependence.

The Enabler. The person who plays this role is usually the spouse. The Enabler feels powerless but desperately tries to hold the family together by controlling family life. He or she is too afraid to express overwhelming feelings of anger. A well-meaning person, the Enabler unwittingly allows and even encourages irresponsible and self-destructive behavior in the Dependent by shielding him or her from the consequences of his or her actions. The payoff for the Enabler is a big one: The person feels self-righteous, responsible, and "important" in striving to keep the family intact. Unfortunately, the stress of playing this role exacts a stiff price: depression, multiple physical illnesses, and sometimes the abuse of alcohol or other chemicals.

The Hero. The Hero believes that by being perfect, responsible, and achieving good grades or bringing pride to the family through accomplishments, the problems in the family will be taken care of. Unfortunately, when the Hero fails, he or she also feels inadequate and guilty. Still, there is some payoff for the Hero. The family feels some worth by looking up to the Hero, who, in turn, is unable to abandon being seen as a Hero. If the Hero tries actually to fix the family problem by confronting it, the situation can go from bad to worse. The rest of the family may change its attitude toward the Hero from one of admiration to blame. Remember, change is uncomfortable. When the Hero does family members the favor of confronting their unhealthy roles, they will feel very uncomfortable and try to return the favor.

The Scapegoat. An older child or teen is usually the first to take on this role. He or she is the person the family blames for its problems. In turn, the Scapegoat feels hurt but is unable to show it. Eventually, he or she will retaliate by breaking major family, school, or community rules. The payoff is that the Scapegoat takes the family attention off the real problem and refocuses it on himself or herself. In the Scapegoat, the family finds an easier target than dealing with the Dependent, who has more power. The Scapegoat often seeks relief by using chemicals or engaging in other anti-social and self-destructive behaviors.

The Lost Child. As older family members take on more powerful unhealthy roles, they will ignore one child, who will gradually become "lost" and fade into the woodwork. As in a tornado, where the smallest objects are thrown the farthest, damaged the most, and discovered the last, so does this phenomenon take place in the turbulence of a chemically dependent family. The Lost Child is alone, shy, withdrawn, feels painfully lonely, but never tells. The payoff for playing this role is that the Lost Child finds an escape from the dangerous winds blowing in the family. The family mistakenly views this member with relief, believing that no news is good news, that at least he or she is not making trouble like everyone else. The role of the Lost Child, however, exacts a high price: He or she is isolated from others. To deal with that profound loneliness, the Lost Child may also later turn to the companionship of alcohol or other drugs or develop some other addictive disorder.

The Mascot. The Mascot role is usually played by the youngest member of the family. He or she becomes the family clown, who takes the focus off the family problem by being cute or funny. The child plays this role because he or she is afraid of the daily eruptions of violence and turmoil. The last child to enter into this chaotic family, the Mascot has not learned how to translate his or her fears into words. The Mascot is also afraid of being rejected by others if he or she speaks about his or her fears. So the Mascot believes that everyone is better off when he or she makes everyone laugh. Of course, this means that no one ever takes the Mascot seriously. The payoff for the Mascot is seeing the family have a little fun and getting a break from painful feelings. The price the Mascot pays is delayed maturity and emotional problems. The Mascot grows up believing that the golden rule of family life is "Don't ever talk about or attempt to solve any problem that makes you feel upset. Just laugh it off and pretend it isn't there."

When family members play these roles for a long period of time, they fall into the deadly trap of believing that they actually *are* the roles they play. They are entangled in behavior that keeps them comfortable and able to cope, but only by being miserable on a feeling level. They believe that life would be much worse if they sought help, so they are actually trapped by a problem that can't be solved.

The way out of this trap for families may seem simple, but you should know that it takes some really hard work. To recover, you and your family need to break out of and abandon your unhealthy roles and create and establish healthy family roles. It's best to get the help of a professional therapist when trying to get out of this trap. However, participation in Al-Anon for adults or Alateen for teenagers can also be very helpful.

To begin, you must learn to tolerate any feeling you experience without blowing up, withdrawing, or falling apart. Feelings, after all, are only feelings. Try to view them as friends who tell you if trouble or happiness are heading your way. Then you can give yourself time to prepare for the best or for the worst.

For example, suppose your teen, who has been free of alcohol and other drugs for six months, wants to borrow the car and stay out past curfew. When you hesitate to grant this request, your youngster throws a whale of a temper tantrum. In the old days, you might have enabled him or her by giving in or making him or her feel guilty. Perhaps you might have matched his or her temper tantrum with one of your own. Now, you realize how angry you feel over your child's self-centeredness, how babyish he or she still can be at times, but how rarely such behavior occurs. So lower your voice. Let your teen know that you understand his or her needs, but that he or she must calm down or nothing will be discussed. Once you have identified and expressed your feelings and encouraged your teen to do the same, you'll be in a much better position to discuss the situation with your teen and arrive at a healthy and mutually acceptable resolution.

Besides learning to tolerate and deal appropriately with your feelings, you also need to learn all you can about the unhealthy role you have been playing. Such knowledge can help you from falling back into the role and putting you and your family back in danger. Likewise, see to it that everyone in your family learns about these roles. Perhaps the best way to do this is to hold family meetings, with or without the help of a therapist, to discuss how family members can forsake old roles.

Creating a Healthy Family Structure

Just as a house needs a foundation, walls, and a roof, so does a family need the healthy structure provided by effective rules and conse-quences and loving authority. Recall how we saw that contracts and recovery plans are the first family tools for securing safety, respect, and trust (stage two, Stability and Structure).

Recovering families need rules to help provide structure to family living. No matter what your family rules are, they must be followed and enforced consistently. In deciding upon rules, the most basic are: (1) no alcohol or other drugs; (2) no violence or threats of violence; (3) respect others' opinions; (4) respect parents' authority; (5) continue to get professional help; and (6) agree to discuss and solve problems. No rule or consequence for breaking a rule should ever restrict a teenager from attending a self-help group or therapy session because it's in these settings that a difficult teen can think out his or her mistakes and learn how to deal with life's problems in a healthy way.

Someone has to be in charge of making decisions and keeping order in the family. Generally, that someone is the parent or parents. In the past, your disruptive child may have run the household. Perhaps your teen intimidated you so much that you lacked the confidence and presence of mind to be seen as—or to function as—the authority. If this is true, you may not be able to take charge that easily if family members don't agree to it. So, you have to work on changing your own unhealthy behavior and on earning trust before family members will respect your authority. It helps if you keep in mind what recovery phase the family is in and is willing to work on the specific recovery tasks that phase entails. Given your hard work, your authority will be eventually recognized, acknowledged, and accepted. In essence, your family will empower you to have power in the family.

As your family continues to recover, your chemically dependent teen will cease trying to wrest power from you by making up his or her own rules. Instead, your teen will recognize that his or her real power comes from building trust that is gained in work and school and other activities, from staying free of alcohol and other drugs, and from building self-confidence.

Maintaining a Healthy Marital Relationship or Maintaining Yourself as a Healthy Single, Divorced, or Remarried Parent

We emphasize this final requirement of recovery because given the trouble, time, and stress parents spend on solving the problems of their chemically dependent teen, their relationships often suffer. Married parents neglect one another in order to deal with their troubled teen. When a family loses or gains a parent, raising a chemically dependent child can be even tougher. Thus, when it comes to family recovery, single parents especially need support, divorced parents especially need control, and remarried parents especially need patience. These coping skills prevent the family from becoming stressed out, chaotic, and disorganized. Parents—*all* parents—who haven't mastered these skills are actually giving their chemically dependent child the opportunity to continue using alcohol or other drugs.

Married Parents. Many married partners are very hard on themselves, believing that they've failed their child and deserve to be punished. Others believe without reason that married life requires little effort on their part for it to go smoothly and may ignore or deny problems with their children. Finally, some parents are just too worn out by their child's troublemaking to give any attention to one another or even to themselves.

Look to expert therapists, clergy, and excellent books on the subject to offer you assistance. Spend time maintaining a healthy marital relationship by sharing feelings and hopes, planning your life together, having fun, keeping your sexual life alive, and sharing in the raising of your children.

Single Parents. Having a partner who can share some of your burden and stay cooler than you in the heat of an argument is a real benefit of marriage. A happily married parent also has someone to pay attention to his or her emotional needs, so that he or she won't depend too much on his or her children to fulfill them. The single mother or father stands alone. That's why he or she really needs someone to act as a buffer, to step between parent and child when there is a fight that won't stop. Given the normal stresses of work, finances, and child care, many single parents have little energy left to try and guide a chemically dependent teen in the right direction all alone.

As a single parent, and even if you've had enough of marriage, you still deserve some help in raising your child. Look to other single parents to find some support. Groups like Parents Without Partners and other parent peer groups offer places where you can socialize, make friends with others who share your struggles, and find some support. Groups such as Big Brothers, Big Sisters, Boys' Clubs, Girls' Clubs, Scouts, religious groups, and athletic teams offer opportunities for your teenager to find the added guidance, advice, support, and even "tough love" of another adult. Finally, your friends, parents, or siblings also may have the time and energy to be sources of support for you and your recovering family.

Divorced Parents. Even if you've been recently divorced, the pain of separation, the disappointment, and the self-doubt can make you want to blame your "ex" or your children for your troubles. Very often, divorced parents of a chemically dependent teen feel out of control. That feeling seems to come with separation and divorce. But you want your family to recover. And for that to happen, you need to stay in control of your role as a parent.

Doing this isn't easy. Give yourself time—a year at the very least—for the painful wound of separation to heal. Refuse to put your children between your "ex" and yourself. Rather, help your child learn how someone can separate, move on, and find healthier relationships. Finally, know that there are excellent counselors, books, and educational series to help you manage these trying times. Seek their help.

Remarried Parents. When you take the important step of remarrying, your new spouse may think that you've either been too easy or too hard on your out-of-control teenager. Either of you can mistakenly believe that the other doesn't know how to deal with a chemically dependent child. Suddenly, instead of beginning your marriage by getting to know each other and having fun together, you find yourselves spending most of your time arguing about how to parent a chemically dependent teen.

Three standards can help remarried parents in their new marriage. First, no one is an expert when it comes to parenting a chemically dependent child. Get some professional help, so that you'll have enough energy left to keep your marriage alive. Second, if you have married into this family, be patient with your spouse and stepchildren. You're probably still considered a stranger by the children. They will learn to listen to you and respect you more if they get to know your positive side first. Third, refrain from using alcohol or other drugs, especially if a child is in the active phase of chemical dependence. Set a good example. There are many exciting ways for newlyweds to enjoy each other's company without the use of chemicals.

COMMUNITY RECOVERY

At first glance, it may seem somewhat odd to consider recovery in terms of the community. Upon reflection, however, it seems clear that the community plays a major role in the recovery of its chemically dependent teenagers and their families. Let's suppose that a chemically dependent teen has been lucky enough to get help in a treatment program and that his or her family has also taken part. Together, the teen and the family are making progress in personal and family recovery. Now, the teen is ready to return home, home to the community: to the school where he or she used to smoke pot; to the mall where he or she shoplifted to get money for alcohol; to the parties where he or she got intoxicated; to the streets where he or she bought crack cocaine.

Will this recovering teen be able to keep his or her life stable and structured, consistent and balanced in a school that may not know how to support his or her recovery or how to give appropriate consequences for alcohol or other drug use at school? Will the youngster be able to manage independence needs and deal with the possibility of a relapse in a neighborhood where law enforcement agencies may be ineffective in dealing with drug dealing and street crime? Will the teen find mature and healthy people outside the family with whom to attach in a community whose advertising and media glamorize and extol those who casually use alcohol and other drugs?

The community is the final barrier to successful recovery that we have to face. Over the last twenty years, our communities have been in chaos due to the epidemic of chemical dependence. In fact, we can safely state that our communities are struggling in the Crisis Control Stage of recovery. Few communities, no matter their racial makeup, economic status, or geographic location, have their acts together about chemical dependence. The problem seems clear but not the solution.

This isn't to say that some communities aren't working to deal with the problem. Indeed, some communities are making valiant efforts to create neighborhoods that protect families and stop our chemical dependence epidemic. In these communities, individuals and groups work together in a variety of ways to empower their children to avoid problems with alcohol and other drugs. A few of these efforts are listed below:

Role Model Organizations. In many communities, concerned adults are devoting their time and energies to help children of low-income families, minorities, and single-parent homes, who lack positive role models or a parent who can show them what it means to be a mature woman or man.

Neighborhood Watch Groups. Neighborhoods and law enforcement have formed partnerships to keep those who prey on our children off the streets and out of the playgrounds.

Parent Involvement in the Schools. Parents are creating all sorts of partnerships with schools that support the ideals of no alcohol or other drug use; solid education; and healthy living. These partnerships protect children from harm and inspire them to learn.

Parental Pledges. Through the auspices of the schools, parents have agreed to list their names as being willing to hold supervised and chemical-free parties for teens in their homes. They also pledge to "stay out of the way" so as not to cramp teens as they party.

Recreational Programs. Cities such as St. Louis, Missouri, and Seattle, Washington, have polled their teenage populations to discover their recreational needs. Not surprisingly, both cities discovered that teens ranked their greatest need as having more places to hang out that were safe from violence and drugs. Adults in authority from both cities are working with teens to provide healthy and exciting places to spend leisure time.

A Greater Variety of Treatment Services. Both private and public mental health care centers across the country are beginning to create new outpatient and inpatient treatment programs that treat chemically dependent teens according to the seriousness of their problems. Both sorts of programs seek to prevent unnecessary hospitalization and to keep down the cost of treatment. Insurance companies and Medicaid are beginning to respond to these treatment innovations by their willingness to reimburse clients.

Efforts like these demonstrate that communities do recognize that they play a crucial role in aiding recovery. More than that, efforts like these empower communities to protect their youngest and most vulnerable members from the devastation caused by chemical dependence. Even more, efforts like these send a signal to all our communities that they can take up the challenge of chemical dependence, empower those who suffer from the disease to recover, empower their children to avoid it, and empower themselves to abolish it.

CONCLUSION

In this book we've explained that a teenager's recovery from chemical dependence is a process of growth and change that is unique to the developing adolescent. This process is ongoing. That is, the teen doesn't *attain* recovery, but is *recovering*. We've seen that the recovering teenager must put forth time and effort to move through each of the four recovery stages. This process will not and cannot take place without the help of professionals, peers, family, and parents.

Your teen may not seek out your help, but he or she desperately needs it. Crippled by the effects of alcohol and other drug use, your child will not succeed on his or her own along the way of recovery. Whether your youngster shows it or not, he or she needs you to walk alongside during this challenging journey of recovery.

Empowering Parents on the Recovery Journey

Throughout this book you've traversed many twists and turns of the journey of recovery. Along the way, you've discovered several aspects of the work you have to do both to ensure your teenager's recovery and to find some personal relief from the pain of your child's chemical dependence. That work can be summarized into six, parent-empowering tasks. You've already encountered these tasks elsewhere throughout this book. They are reviewed here to give you a brief profile for personal empowerment.

Parent-Empowering Tasks

1. Detach yourself from your teenager's chemical dependence.
2. Keep your authority as a parent by setting limits that any healthy teenager should follow.
3. Problem solve instead of panicking or looking to blame someone else for your troubles.
4. Admit how you've been responsible both for keeping your family healthy and for hurting your family and yourself.
5. Work to fulfill your lifelong goals.
6. Maintain a sense of humor.

Attending to these tasks will empower you to make a great difference in your child's journey of recovery, help to prevent relapse, and offer you the support you need to continue the journey.

Detach Yourself

As you've already seen, the word "detachment" has a very special meaning when it relates to your youngster's chemical dependence. It means that while you remain responsible to your teen as a parent, you are not responsible *for* him or her. For example, as a parent you provide a safe, secure environment for your child. You are being responsible to him or her. However, if your teenager gets into trouble with the law, your child must experience the consequences of his or her actions, even if it means going to jail. It's not your job to protect your child from the consequences of his or her own actions. If you do, your child will never learn to be a responsible human being and that all actions have consequences, good and bad.

Completing the task of detaching yourself from your teenager's chemical dependence has two important results. First, it gives your youngster a chance to learn the fundamental life skills (for example, problem solving) needed for recovery. Second, it protects you as a parent by preventing you from getting pulled into your child's negative patterns of behavior.

Set Limits

One of the primary duties of all parents is to set limits for their children. The smallest infant is naturally geared to exploring the big, mysterious world around it. As a parent, you should encourage this, for it will become a lifelong quest. At the same time, you have to set limits to protect your child's safety and health. You don't let a baby put its hand on a hot stove to learn about heat. Likewise, you don't let your teenager take the car if he or she is drunk. Neither is safe.

When you set limits, make sure that they are clear and appropriate, and that you enforce them. Sometimes it helps to write them down and discuss them with your teenager until you are sure that he or she understands. Remember, a limit should also be appropriate to your child's needs and capacities. For instance, if your teenager is newly sober, it is appropriate not to allow him or her to associate with drug-using friends because of the risk and temptation involved. Later, as your teen progresses in his or her recovery, your youngster will gradually learn that to remain sober he or she needs to find new friends who won't invite a return to drug-using behavior.

Like any teen, your chemically dependent teenager will test your limits more and more as he or she reaches for independence. But no matter how much your child questions or tests your limits, know that your teen needs them and, in fact, relies on them. Be fair but firm.

Problem Solve

This task means that you must realize that your child is sick and needs your help. If a peer introduced your teen to alcohol or other drugs, he or she is certainly not going to let your youngster get and stay sober. Nor is that peer's parents' responsibility to help your child. You must face this challenge as loving parents who want to see your teenager recover and feel good about life and himself or herself again. Remember, however, that you are not alone in this task. Don't be afraid to rely on friends, family, and caring professionals to help you with the decisions you have to face and the problems you have to solve.

Admit Responsibility

As a parent, you have a responsibility to help your family stay healthy. If your child breaks a bone or suffers from some illness, you should engage the help of a professional physician. If your child suffers from the disease of chemical dependence, you should also find appropriate treatment. Acting this way, parents acknowledge that they are indeed accountable for their family's health.

Sometimes, however, the task of admitting responsibility means that parents may need to acknowledge that they have played a role in hurting themselves or other family members. For example, a parent who is chemically dependent is emotionally absent for a child. That child may assume parental duties, like fixing meals or getting younger siblings off to school. In such a case, the parent needs to admit that he or she has neglected to be responsible for family health, and in fact, is responsible for family disorder.

When you assume your responsibility for either maintaining or inhibiting a healthy family, you go a long way in strengthening your teenager's recovery.

Fulfill Lifelong Goals

When you discover that your teenager is chemically dependent, you may think that your life is ruined. Your life will be different, no question about it. But you don't have to admit defeat, relinquish your dreams, and expect nothing more out of your life. As your teenager begins the process of recovery, don't lose sight of your own life and the goals you've set for yourself. Healthy detachment will help you keep these goals in mind and in perspective.

So, if your plans to pursue further education were interrupted because of your child's chemical dependence, now is the time to resume those plans. If you've lost a lot of time at work because of the problems related to your teenager's chemical dependence, begin to show some renewed interest in your job and in taking on more responsibilities. If you've lost touch with your other children because your focus has been on the child struggling with alcohol or other drugs, reestablish those bonds by giving your other children what they haven't had from you lately—your time and attention.

Undertake this task, and you'll be pleasantly surprised to see that your goals are attainable. Discovering this can bring new hope and meaning to your life.

Maintain a Sense of Humor

Always, always remember to laugh once in awhile. Chemical dependence is serious business, just as is your child's recovery. Even so, there are moments in all of the chaos and pain you're going through that may strike you as funny and make you laugh. Go ahead, let it out. Humor is an excellent way to forgive the feelings of others. Humor also leads to hope, which is something you'll need as your teenager recovers.

This book has had a lot to say about chemically dependent teenagers and their recovery. But this book was not written for your teen. It was written for you. As parents of a chemically dependent adolescent, the recovery journey you're on is not a comfortable one. It makes many demands upon its travelers. Hazards, road blocks, and dangerous curves mark its way. As you proceed, you'll find yourselves lost now and then, longing for a safe refuge. Know that there is such a haven, that there is shelter from the storm you've been enduring. As your teen recovers, so will you. Meanwhile, be patient with yourselves. Empower yourselves. And go firmly but gently, one step at a time.

THE TWELVE STEPS OF ALCOHOLICS ANONYMOUS[8]

1. We admitted that we were powerless over alcohol—that our lives had become unmanageable.

2. Came to believe that a Power greater than ourselves could restore us to sanity.

3. Made a decision to turn our will and our lives over to the care of God *as we understood Him.*

4. Made a searching and fearless moral inventory of ourselves.

5. Admitted to God, to ourselves, and to another human being the exact nature of our wrongs.

6. Were entirely ready to have God remove all these defects of character.

7. Humbly asked Him to remove our shortcomings.

8. Made a list of all persons we had harmed, and became willing to make amends to them all.

9. Made direct amends to such people wherever possible, except when to do so would injure them or others.

10. Continued to take personal inventory and when we were wrong promptly admitted it.

11. Sought through prayer and meditation to improve our conscious contact with God *as we understood Him,* praying only for knowledge of His will for us and the power to carry that out.

12. Having had a spiritual awakening as a result of these steps, we tried to carry this message to alcoholics, and to practice these principles in all our affairs.

[8] From *Alcoholics Anonymous,* Third Edition (New York: Alcoholics Anonymous World Services, Inc., 1976), pp. 59-60. Reprinted with permission of Alcoholics Anonymous World Services, Inc.

THE TWELVE STEPS OF AL-ANON[9]

1. We admitted that we were powerless over alcohol—that our lives had become unmanageable.

2. Came to believe that a Power greater than ourselves could restore us to sanity.

3. Made a decision to turn our will and our lives over to the care of God *as we understood Him.*

4. Made a searching and fearless moral inventory of ourselves.

5. Admitted to God, to ourselves, and to another human being the exact nature of our wrongs.

6. Were entirely ready to have God remove all these defects of character.

7. Humbly asked Him to remove our shortcomings.

8. Made a list of all persons we had harmed, and became willing to make amends to them all.

9. Made direct amends to such people wherever possible, except when to do so would injure them or others.

10. Continued to take personal inventory and when we were wrong promptly admitted it.

11. Sought through prayer and meditation to improve our conscious contact with God *as we understood Him,* praying only for knowledge of His will for us and the power to carry that out.

12. Having had a spiritual awakening as a result of these steps, we tried to carry this message to others, and to practice these principles in all our affairs.

---

[9] From *Al-Anon Faces Alcoholism*, Second Edition (New York: Al-Anon Family Headquarters, Inc., 1989), pp. 236-237. Note that Al-Anon has adapted these steps from Alcoholics Anonymous with only minor changes, viz., Step 12.

FOR FURTHER READING

You can find most of these books at your local library or bookstore. If you have any trouble finding them, you can call the following mail order publishers toll-free and also be sent a free catalog:

THE JOHNSON INSTITUTE:	1-800-231-5165
In Minnesota, call:	1-800-247-0484
In Canada, call:	1-800-447-6660
COMPCARE PUBLISHERS:	1-800-328-3330
In Minnesota, call:	1-612-559-4800 (collect)

BOOKS ON ADOLESCENT CHEMICAL DEPENDENCE AND PARENTING

Dupont, Robert L. *Getting Tough on Gateway Drugs: A Guide for the Family.* Washington D.C.: American Psychiatric Press, 1984.

Schaefer, Dick. *Choices & Consequences: What to Do When a Teenager Uses Drugs/Alcohol, A Step-by-Step System That Really Works.* Minneapolis, Minn.: Johnson Institute, 1987.

Wilmes, David J. *Parenting for Prevention: How to Raise a Child to Say No to Alcohol/Drugs.* Minneapolis, Minn.: Johnson Institute, 1988.

York, Phyllis, York, David and Wachtel, Ted. *Toughlove.* Garden City, New York: Doubleday & Co., 1982.

BOOKS ON PERSONAL AND FAMILY RECOVERY

Beattie, Melody. *Co-Dependent No More: How to Stop Controlling Others and Start Caring for Yourself.* Minneapolis, Minn.: Hazelden, 1987.

Black, Claudia. *It Will Never Happen To Me.* Denver, Colo.: Medical Administration, 1980.

Bradshaw, John. *Healing the Shame That Binds You.* Pompano Beach, Fla.: Health Communications, Inc., 1988.

Cermak, Timmen. *A Time to Heal: The Road to Recovery for Adult Children of Alcoholics.* New York: Avon Books, 1989.

Gorski, Terence. *Learning to Live Again: A Guide to Recovery From Addiction and Drug Dependence.* Independence, Mo.: Independence Press, 1982.

Gorski, Terence and Miller, Merlene. *Staying Sober: A Guide for Relapse Prevention.* Independence, Mo.: Independence Press, 1986.

Hayes, Jody. *Smart Love: A Co-Dependence Recovery Program.* Los Angeles, Calif.: J. P. Parcher, Inc., 1989.

Johnson, Vernon. *Intervention: How to Help Someone Who Doesn't Want Help.* Minneapolis, Minn.: Johnson Institute, 1986.

Kritsberg, Wayne. *The Adult Children of Alcoholics Syndrome: From Discovery to Recovery.* Pompano Beach, Fla.: Health Communications, Inc., 1985.

Wegscheider-Cruse, Sharon. *Another Chance: Hope for Health for the Alcoholic Family.* Revised Edition. Palo Alto, Calif.: Science and Behavior Books, 1990.

Wegscheider-Cruse, Sharon. *Choicemaking: For Co-Dependents, Adult Children and Spirituality Seekers.* Pompano Beach, Fla.: Health Communications, Inc., 1985.

Whitfield, Charles L. *Healing the Child Within: Discovery and Recovery for Adult Children of Dysfunctional Families.* Pompano Beach, Fla.: Health Communications, Inc., 1987.

Woititz, Janet G. *Adult Children of Alcoholics.* Pompano Beach, Fla.: Health Communications, Inc., 1983.

FURTHER READING

Books

Conducting Support Groups for Students Affected by Chemical Dependence by Martin Fleming.

Healing the Hurt: Rebuilding Relationships with Your Children, A Self-Help Guide for Parents in Recovery by Rosalie Cruise Jesse, Ph.D.

Everything You Need to Know About Chemical Dependence: Vernon Johnson's Complete Guide for Families by Vernon E. Johnson, D.D.

Intervention: How to Help Someone Who Doesn't Want Help—A Step-by-Step Guide for Families and Friends of Chemically Dependent Persons by Vernon E. Johnson, D.D.

Diagnosing and Treating Co-dependence: A Guide for Professionals Who Work with Chemical Dependents, Their Spouses, and Children by Timmen L. Cermak, M.D.

Different Like Me: A Book for Teens Who Worry About Their Parents' Use of Alcohol/Drugs by Evelyn Leite and Pamela Espeland.

Choices & Consequences: What to Do When a Teenager Uses Alcohol/Drugs by Dick Schaefer.

Parenting for Prevention: How to Raise a Child to Say No to Alcohol/Drugs by David Wilmes.

When Chemicals Come to School: The Student Assistance Program Manual by Gary L. Anderson.

Treating Chemically Dependent Families. A Practical Approach for Professionals by John T. Edwards, Ph.D.

Conducting Support Groups for Elementary Children K-6 by Jerry Moe and Peter Ways.

Booklets

Anger: How to Handle It During Recovery by Becky Sisco

Alcoholism: A Treatable Disease

Chemical Dependence: Yes, You Can Do Something

Why Haven't I Been Able to Help?

The Family Enablers

How It Feels to Be Chemically Dependent by Evelyn Leite

Chemical Dependence and Recovery: A Family Affair

Detachment vs. Intervention: Is There a Conflict?

Detachment: The Art of Letting Go While Living with an Alcoholic by Evelyn Leite

Recovery of Chemically Dependent Families

Enabling in the School Setting by Gary L. Anderson

Solving Alcohol/Drug Problems in Your School by Gary L. Anderson

A Job Description for Parents by David Wilmes

A Job Description for Kids by David Wilmes

Helping Kids Understand Their Feelings by David Wilmes

Helping Kids Communicate by David Wilmes

Helping Kids Learn Refusal Skills by David Wilmes

Is Your Child Involved with Alcohol and Other Drugs? by Dick Schaefer

Workbooks

Can I Handle Alcohol/Drugs? A Self-Assessment Guide for Youth by David Zarek and James Sipe

Breaking Away: Saying Good-bye to Alcohol/Drugs; A Guide to Help Teenagers Stop Using Chemicals by Jean Sassatelli, R.N.

How to Stay Clean and Sober: A Relapse Prevention Guide for Teenagers by Martin Fleming

Films/Videocassettes

Back to Reality: Color, 33 minutes

Enabling: Masking Reality: Color, 22 minutes

Intervention: Facing Reality: Color, 30 minutes

Choices and Consequences: Intervention with Youth in Trouble with Alcohol/Drugs: Color, 33 minutes

The Mirror of a Child: Color, 30 minutes

Different Like Me: Color, 30 minutes

Twee, Fiddle and Huff: Color, 16 minutes (animation)

For more information, or to order any of these publications, films, or videocassettes call toll-free:

Johnson Institute
1-800-231-5165
In Minnesota, call 1-800-247-0484 or 944-0511
In Canada, call 1-800-447-6660

When ordering, be sure to request copies of Johnson Institute's annual catalog.

GROUPS AND ORGANIZATIONS

The following groups and organizations can provide additional information on preventing alcohol/drug use by children and adolescents.

A.A.
Alcoholics Anonymous
General Service Office
P. O. Box 459
Grand Central Station
New York, NY 10163
(212) 686-1100

Addiction Research Foundation
33 Russell Street
Toronto, Ontario M5S 2S1
(416) 595-6056

Al-Anon Family Group
Headquarters
1372 Broadway
New York, NY 10018-0862
(212) 302-7240

Alateen
1372 Broadway
New York, NY 10018-0862
(212) 302-7240

American Council for Drug
Education
204 Monroe Street
Rockville, MD 20850
(301) 294-0600

Chemical People Project
WQED-TV
4802 Fifth Avenue
Pittsburgh, PA 15213
(412) 622-1491

COAF
Children of Alcoholics
Foundation, Inc.
P. O. Box 4185
New York, NY 10163
(212) 754-0656

Families Anonymous
World Service Office
P. O. Box 528
Van Nuys, CA 91408
(818) 989-7841

Johnson Institute
7205 Ohms Lane
Minneapolis, MN 55439-2159
1-800-231-5165

NACOA
National Association for Children
of Alcoholics, Inc.
31582 Coast Highway
Suite B
South Laguna, CA 92677-3044
(714) 499-3889

Narcotics Anonymous
World Service Office, Inc.
P. O. Box 999
Van Nuys, CA 91409
(818) 780-3951

National Coalition for the Prevention of
Drug and Alcohol Abuse
537 Jones Road
Granville, OH 43023
(614) 587-2800

National Federation of Parents for
Drug-Free Youth
8730 Georgia Avenue
Suite 200
Silver Spring, MD 20910
(301) 585-5437

NCA
National Council on Alcoholism, Inc.
12 West 21st Street
7th Floor
New York, NY 10010
1-800-NCA-CALL

NCADI
National Clearinghouse for
Alcohol/Drug Information
P. O. Box 2345
Rockville, MD 20852
(301) 468-2600

NIAAA
National Institute on Alcohol
Abuse and Alcoholism
Room 16-105, Parklawn Bldg.
5600 Fishers Lane
Rockville, MD 20857
(301) 443-3885

NIDA
National Institute on Drug Abuse
Room 10-05, Parklawn Bldg.
5600 Fishers Lane
Rockville, MD 20857
(301) 443-6480

PRIDE
National Parents Resource
Institute on Drug Education
Robert W. Woodruff Volunteer
Service Center, Suite 1002
100 Edgewood Avenue
Atlanta, GA 30303
(404) 651-2548

SADD
Students Against Drunk Driving
P. O. Box 800
277 Main Street
Marlboro, MA 01752
1-800-521-SADD

Note: Many more resources are available to parents in most communities across the United States. For example, the following organizations are involved in activities to prevent the early use of alcohol/drugs: Girl Scouts of America, Inc., Girls Clubs, Boys Clubs, Lions Clubs International, Kiwanis, 4-H, Freemasons, American Academy of Pediatrics, American Academy of Family Physicians, American Bar Association, and many more.